Rainy Day Ready

ALA Public Programs Office

Rainy Day Ready

Financial
LITERACY
Programs and Tools

EDITED BY MELANIE WELCH AND PATRICK HOGAN

ALA
Editions
CHICAGO   2020

MELANIE WELCH is a project director in the ALA Public Programs Office. Melanie is a veteran nonprofit professional with experience in outcomes-based work at museums and environmental organizations and expertise in informal education, public programs, and community engagement and outreach. In her current role with ALA's Public Programs Office, she develops informal education programs and professional development opportunities for libraries and library staff of all types throughout the United States. She received a bachelor of science degree in environmental biology from Bradley University and a master of science degree in biology from Northern Illinois University and is a member of the Second Nature class of Catto Fellows at the Aspen Institute.

PATRICK HOGAN is an editor with the American Library Association's book publishing imprint. Previously, he was an editor with a Chicago business book publisher.

© 2020 by the American Library Association

Extensive effort has gone into ensuring the reliability of the information in this book; however, the publisher makes no warranty, express or implied, with respect to the material contained herein.

ISBN: 978-0-8389-4631-2 (paper)

Library of Congress Control Number: 2019041464

Cover design by Kimberly Thornton. Composition by Alejandra Diaz in the Charis SIL, Brandon Grotesque, Rift Soft and Pauline typefaces.

♾ This paper meets the requirements of ANSI/NISO Z39.48-1992 (Permanence of Paper).

Printed in the United States of America
24 23 22 21 20   5 4 3 2 1

CONTENTS

PREFACE

oney: everybody's thinking about it, but no one wants to talk about it. According to Capital Group, US adults say they would rather talk about marital conflicts, mental illness, drug addiction, politics, and religion before broaching the topic of money.

At the same time, financial literacy is vital to a person's success and well-being. Many life events—from graduating high school, to making decisions about one's health, to getting married or divorced—require a firm grasp of personal finance. Imagine trying to buy a home without a basic understanding of mortgages or aging without a plan for retirement income. People in these situations find themselves not only in dire financial situations but also at a high risk of being defrauded.

As we have seen, the marketplace alone should not be trusted to teach these skills; the Great Recession from December 2007 to June 2009 reminded us what can happen when the marketplace leads consumers down a problematic path.

Libraries—valued, trusted local institutions—can fill the gap.

Your collection is helpful for the self-learner, but books don't reach all demographics equally. Unfortunately, publishing in personal finance tends to target the middle class and more affluent individuals; the most popular books peddle dreams of investment riches or financial independence distant from most people's everyday reality.

In this book, we suggest that library programming is the solution. Luckily, there are numerous trustworthy resources to make library workers' jobs easier in this regard—if you know where to look.

The Financial Industry Regulatory Authority (FINRA) Investor Education Foundation aims to "empower underserved Americans with the knowledge, skills and tools to make sound financial decisions throughout life."[1] The Consumer Financial Protection Bureau (CFPB) offers libraries free training and print and online outreach materials. Money Smart Week, an initiative of the Chicago Federal Reserve, now boasts more than 2,500 partners in forty-one states, many of them libraries. These organizations and resources are just the tip of the iceberg.

With the goal of helping you get started in financial literacy programming, this book pulls together resources from the American Library Association (ALA), expertise from business librarians, and model programs selected by ALA's Public Programs Office. Adults aren't the only age group that can benefit from this learning; as the programs in this book show, the learning can start as early as preschool.

We thank Kathy Rosa, Michael Dowling, the Reference and User Services Association, its Business Reference and Services Section (BRASS), and its Financial Literacy Interest Group for input and contributions.

NOTE

1. "General Grant Program," FINRA Investor Education Foundation, https://www.finra foundation.org/general-grant-program.

PART I

Libraries

Chapter 1

Supporting Patrons in Financial Decision-Making

LAUREN REITER

Business and Economics Librarian

Penn State University Libraries, University Park, Pennsylvania

"Should I buy or lease a car?" "How will I cover an emergency medical bill?" "Should I switch careers?" Whether or not they ask them at the reference desk, library patrons have financial questions that need answers. Financial decision-making and planning are complicated and sensitive topics for both patrons and librarians. Patrons may hesitate to ask for help in finding information about money problems when it is most needed due to feelings of confusion and vulnerability. Librarians may hesitate for similar reasons, such as patron privacy, lack of the financial credentials required to offer advice, and their own comfort level with personal finance topics. Despite these barriers, the questions are inevitable, and the answers have a serious impact on financial lives, particularly at points of transition and change, making it important for libraries to explore ways to help patrons address these challenges.

Although personal finance issues are undeniably personal, this chapter will provide an overview of some key stages marked by important decisions with financial consequences. With increased awareness and sensitivity to the financial side of patrons' lives, librarians can identify new opportunities to connect and support financial decision-making and planning with trusted resources and programs.

CAREER AND EDUCATION DECISIONS

"What do you want to be when you grow up?" Questions about career choice start at an early age and continue through adulthood, especially when choosing a career path and navigating changes along the way. Career exploration may begin with ability, personality, and passion, but the link between work and money means that financial questions will arise. For example, an individual selecting a career path that requires trade school, college, or additional training and certification will need to consider if savings, scholarships, grants, or loans are available to cover the costs of additional education. According to the Federal Reserve's "Report on the Economic Well-Being of U.S. Households in 2017," 42 percent of those who attended college financed at least some of their education using federal student loans, private student loans, credit cards, or other forms of debt.[1] If they must borrow funds to cover educational expenses, which is the growing trend, the individual then needs to consider the following financial questions: What form of debt? How much? What interest rate? One answer begets another question, demonstrating the domino effect of financial decisions.

Children, young adults, and their parents may be among those most likely to encounter career- and education-related financial questions. They will be eager to learn about career possibilities, postsecondary education options, college savings plans, student loans, and completing a Free Application for Federal Student Aid (FAFSA). Those returning to school or changing careers may also be interested in career exploration resources, education financing options, cover letter and résumé writing, and interview skills. A library is well positioned to meet these needs through resources and programming. For example, through government resources such as the Bureau of Labor Statistics' *Occupational Outlook Handbook*, the library and librarian can facilitate access to salary data, which can inform financial decision-making in situations ranging from negotiating wages with an employer to determining how much to take out in student loans based on anticipated postgraduation salary. Libraries can also develop career collections with books on job application materials, guides to college majors and professions, and databases such as Vault, which includes company reviews and rankings, job and industry information, career advice, and job postings. Related topics for library financial literacy programming and workshops include tips for the job hunt, information on the FAFSA, scholarship lists, company and industry research for interview preparation and salary negotiation, and other career and postsecondary education exploration topics.

See the program models "Harry Potter and the Prisoner of Student Debt" (chapter 12) and the speaker panel of "Planning for Life after High School" (chapter 13).

MANAGING DEBT AND CREDIT

"Is debt good or bad?" Because student loans are valued as a way of investing in one's self, leading to enhanced knowledge and earnings, and improving worth over time, they are often referred to as *good debt*. Mortgages fall into this category as well. Automotive loans and credit card debt are examples of so-called bad debt because the assets they are used to purchase are typically depreciating. Taking on any form of debt, good or bad, leads to questions about interest rates, payment schedules, and comparison shopping. Consumers face questions about whether or not the asset or product they are purchasing is worth the value they will get out of it and if there are other options on the market. Patrons in pursuit of large purchases also need to consider whether their credit score is high enough to qualify for the loan that they seek at the rate that they want, inviting new questions about FICO versus VantageScore, the components of a credit score, hard and soft inquiries, and how to improve bad credit. Some library patrons may also lack a credit history or bank account. According to the "2017 FDIC National Survey of Unbanked and Underbanked Households," 20 percent of US households have little to no credit history, 6.5 percent are unbanked, and 18.7 are underbanked, meaning that they have a bank account but also use alternative financial services, such as money orders, check cashing, and payday loans.[2]

Financial decisions related to the various forms of household debt begin as soon as an individual has his or her own buying power or influence on purchases, meaning these questions start to arise at an early age. Children and young adults could benefit from education on media and advertising as well as introductions to core financial literacy concepts, helping them become savvy savers and spenders. The need for education continues for those transitioning into adulthood and older age as the purchases become more expensive. Libraries can support patrons with managing their debt and credit and being a conscious consumer. They can promote authoritative, unbiased, freely available resources. For example, the CFPB offers the "Ask CFPB" reference tool on its website with objective answers to common consumer questions such as "How do I dispute a charge on my credit card bill?" and "What should I do when a debt collector contacts me?" The National Endowment for Financial Education's Smart about Money site provides online courses, tools, and responses to frequently asked money questions like "I need a loan—what are my credit options?" The Federal Reserve Bank of St. Louis offers an array of financial education resources for all ages, including materials educating consumers about the pros and cons of alternative financial services. In addition to promoting free resources for debt and credit management, libraries can provide access to subscriptions like *Consumer Reports* that can be used to review products and evaluate big-ticket purchases. Libraries can also connect patrons with debt and credit counselors and offer workshops about banking basics, planning for a big purchase, buying or leasing a car, buying or renting a home, differentiating between wants and needs, and building and maintaining credit.

See the program models "Smart Cookie Credit" (chapter 17), "You Have Expensive Taste" (chapter 10), and "Money Smart Week at a Community College" (chapter 15).

EMERGENCIES

"But could I cover a big expense I did not expect?" Sometimes planning for a large purchase is not an option. Emergencies and unexpected circumstances arise, often with significant financial consequences. According to the Federal Reserve's "Report on the Economic Well-Being of U.S. Households," 40 percent of adults would not be able to cover an unexpected $400 expense without borrowing money or selling something. The study also found that one in four adults skipped doctor's visits, dental needs, prescription medicine, mental health care or counseling, and other medical treatments because they could not afford the costs.[3] Without an emergency fund, people have little to protect themselves in the event of an unexpected job loss, medical bill, or natural disaster, such as a flood or hurricane. In these situations, which are punctuated by personal and emotional strife, financial trouble is the last thing anyone would want to worry about but is the dismal reality. Investment fraud, identify theft, data breaches, financial exploitation, and other financial crimes provide additional examples of the unexpected and unwanted financial troubles patrons may encounter.

Although a crisis can strike anyone and wreak havoc on his or her finances, certain populations may be more vulnerable depending on the type of emergency. For example, the FBI warns that senior citizens are a primary target of fraudsters because they are more likely to have savings and good credit, tend to value trust and politeness, and often make poor witnesses, if they report the crime at all.[4] Various government agencies, such as the CFPB and the Federal Trade Commission, produce useful tools for librarians and patrons. For example, the CFPB offers the "Money Smart for Older Americans" print guide as well as an overview of common fraud schemes including lottery and prize scams, debt collection and relief scams, and wire and money transfer fraud. Federal Trade Commission resources include IdentityTheft.gov, which could be used to walk a patron through reporting identity theft and developing a plan for recovering from harm. For natural disasters, FEMA's Ready.gov provides the emergency financial first aid kit, which covers the steps to financial preparedness, such as safeguarding insurance policies and financial documents and updating paperwork regularly. FEMA's materials also cover assistance resources in the event of a disaster and steps to protecting oneself against scams targeting disaster survivors. In addition to informational resources, libraries can connect patrons with programs on building an emergency fund, health and home insurance, unemployment assistance, and financial exploitation awareness. Experts to present on these topics may be found in local banks and credit unions, insurance agencies, police departments, and government offices. Throughout crisis prevention and recovery, libraries can serve as safe havens of understanding and support while individuals determine their next steps.

See the program model "Starting Over" (chapter 19).

PLANNING FOR THE FUTURE

"Will I ever be able to retire?" The FINRA Investor Education Foundation report *Financial Capability in the United States 2016* found that 39 percent of Americans have attempted to determine how much they will need to save for retirement and 56 percent have not.[5] For long-term financial decision-making and planning, patrons may be considering their general retirement goals or have specific investment questions on stocks, bonds, and mutual funds. They may find themselves wondering how much to save toward retirement or other long-term goals and what investment vehicles to select. In planning for the future, individuals may also be thinking about people beyond themselves, perhaps immediate family members or philanthropic community causes. Patrons may be considering their responsibilities in caring for children or older parents and the financial needs of those circumstances. Some may find themselves as part of the *sandwich generation*, with financial caregiving responsibilities to both their parents and children at once. Membership in the sandwich generation may increase over time. Nearly 80 percent of parents give some type of financial support to their adult children, leading financial newspaper *Barron's* to ask the provocative question, "Will your kids ruin your retirement?"[6] Patrons' financial futures are complicated by their present circumstances, and libraries can help with navigating the complexities.

Individuals confront their financial futures at different stages of life. Some may start thinking about their investments when they get their first job that comes with a 401(k) plan. Others may not start thinking about saving until retirement is an impending reality. In still other cases, the best-laid plans are forced in a new direction when unanticipated needs, such as financial caregiving, arise. In all cases, libraries are positioned to provide people with the tools and information to address complex financial planning. Librarians can guide patrons to freely available online guides for investment education. For example, FINRA Investor Education Foundation provides investor news alerts, online fund analyzers, market data, tools for researching brokerage firms, and other investor education materials. The Securities and Exchange Commission's Investor.gov site includes an introduction to investing, guidance on questions to explore and research to do before investing, and compound interest calculators and other financial planning tools. Libraries can also provide access to financial information databases and resources from Morningstar, Value Line, Mergent, and Standard & Poor's and develop collections of books and newspapers covering investing and financial markets. Libraries can also offer a wide range of programming to help patrons with financial planning—including workshops on financial goal setting, retirement savings, financial caregiving, and investment research—and hosting sessions by certified financial planners, bankers, accountants, and other financial professionals.

CONCLUSION

This overview of common life transitions and their associated financial challenges is not exhaustive, and every community has different needs. Broadly speaking, the key to identifying other critical life stages and their related financial questions is to look for changes in the lives of library patrons. For example, when an individual moves to a new city or country, he or she experiences not only major geographic and cultural shifts but also significant financial changes, ranging from budgeting to match the cost of living in a new city to learning a new process for completing local or federal taxes.

See the program model "Financial Literacy for New Americans" (chapter 14).

Librarians on the lookout for major life transitions will be able to identify the need and find opportunities to support patrons' financial decision-making and planning through those changes.

NOTES

1. Board of Governors of the Federal Reserve System, "Report on the Economic Well-Being of U.S. Households in 2017," 2018, www.federalreserve.gov/publications/report -economic-well-being-us-households.htm.

2. Federal Deposit Insurance Corporation, "2017 FDIC National Survey of Unbanked and Underbanked Households," 2018, www.fdic.gov/householdsurvey/2017/2017report.pdf.

3. Federal Reserve System, "Report on the Economic Well-Being."

4. Federal Bureau of Investigation, "Fraud against Seniors," www.fbi.gov/scams-and-safety/common-fraud-schemes/seniors.

5. Judy T. Lin et al., *Financial Capability in the United States 2016* (Washington, DC: Finra Investor Education Foundation, 2016), https://www.usfinancialcapability.org/downloads/NFCS_2015_Report_Natl_Findings.pdf.

6. R. Kapadia, "The Parent Trap," *Barron's* 99, no. 12 (2019): 24–25, 27–28, 30. http://ezaccess.libraries.psu.edu/login?url=https://search.proquest.com/docview/2196467555?accountid=13158.

Chapter 2

Gaps and Barriers in the Popular Personal Finance Literature

◇◇

ASH E. FAULKNER

Business Librarian

The Ohio State University Libraries, Columbus, Ohio

I am blessed to be among the readership popular personal finance literature aims to address: I'm employed with benefits; my income is sufficient to cover all my imminent needs, if not my wants; and I worry about things like my "rainy day" fund and my retirement accounts. Many are not so lucky. In a sense, if you cannot afford to buy a popular personal finance book, full price, hardcover . . . it might not be for you.

As I discuss "popular personal finance literature," it is fair to point out that I'm making generalizations and that, like all generalizations, these statements do not apply to *all* books in this genre. Namely, I'm making these generalizations based on a set of twelve titles I read for an article published in the *Journal of Librarianship and Information Science*.[1] This is a small subset of the much larger genre, but I believe it is a subset that is indicative of the genre as a whole. The authors of these titles are names like Suze Orman and Dave Ramsey, names that have wide recognition in popular culture even beyond personal finance. Though, of course, that recognition is not universal. It is part of the problematic nature of the genre that if you don't already recognize the names of the major authors, the books may not be applicable to your situation.

THE EXCLUSIVE NATURE OF POPULAR PERSONAL FINANCE LITERATURE

Namely, the difficulty of popular personal finance literature is that it is to some extent exclusive. It aims to address the average individual or family, which, in the United States, is generally assumed to be a "middle-class" readership. Regardless of whether or not the average financial situation is the *most common* financial situation, the bigger problem with this assumed audience is that the middle class is not the *only* class. Libraries, which have a strong professional emphasis on providing equitable access to information, need to be aware of the fact that, though this genre is an essential part of any financial literacy collection, it should not be the only access point for patrons, as it will leave many at the gate.

Personal finance literature focuses mainly on addressing short-term financial comfort and long-term financial needs. Ultimately, these are luxury concerns. Debating, for instance, whether one's career should be personally fulfilling or just maximize one's income so one can be personally fulfilled with more free time or an earlier retirement is a question of self-actualization. On Maslow's hierarchy of needs, this is the pinnacle. What about those for whom finances are a more imminent question of physiological needs? What about people with questions of short-term financial need for whom long-term financial questions cannot yet even be contemplated?

BARRIERS TO ACCESSING POPULAR PERSONAL FINANCE LITERATURE

Partially because of this assumed audience, popular personal finance literature also has a number of very real barriers to accessing its content. First, a reader must have a high level of reading skills. To be fair, this is a potential barrier to access for most adult educational titles. But in addition, popular personal finance literature requires a reader to possess the following:

- some preexisting knowledge of basic financial concepts and products
- a steady current income stream
- access to financial products (if one is to follow given advice)

- enough confidence to enact financial decisions once made
- a very definite and disciplined desire to learn about personal finance

As to the first barrier, the texts universally assume, for instance, that readers have bank accounts and debit cards, and instead of discussing the advantages of banking and how to obtain an account, they instead dive into debates regarding credit cards, financing major purchases like homes and cars and/or automating one's finances. The "2017 FDIC National Survey of Unbanked and Underbanked Households" reported that 6.5 percent of US households were unbanked in 2017, with an additional 18.7 percent *underbanked* (households that have at least one bank account holder but also used alternative financial services such as payday loans in the past twelve months).[2] This means that more than 20 percent of US households would likely benefit from a discussion of the most basic financial products available and the benefits and trade-offs of utilizing alternative financial services. These are not frequent features of popular personal finance texts.

Most of the personal finance literature also assumes its readers have a steady income stream in that the discussions and recommendations for action usually focus on things like steady debt repayment and dollar-cost averaging investing. Pundits debate, for instance, paying down various debts based on the charged interest rates (highest to lowest) or via the *snowball method* (wherein you pay off debts based on the amount of debt, smallest to largest, to build psychological momentum). Both sides of the debate though assume one is making steady payments. Dollar-cost averaging, which is exhorted in multiple texts, refers to the fact that if you buy into an investment such as a mutual fund steadily, your dollars will buy more or fewer shares based on the cost of the shares at any given point in time, but over time, you will end up buying more shares at a lower cost than if you bought in a single lump-sum investment. An individual cannot take advantage of dollar-cost averaging if he or she does not have a steady stream of funds to invest. To these individuals, this frequent discussion in the literature is moot. In automating one's finances, which is a popular topic, a regular income stream is *essential.* One cannot have expenses drawn automatically from one's bank account if one's account doesn't have equally automatic and regular inputs. If one's income stream is unstable or currently nonexistent, none of this advice is applicable. Personal finance texts tend to focus less on how to obtain a steady active income stream and instead take this as a given prerequisite.

In order to actually carry out much of the advice given in popular personal finance literature, one would need access to the various financial products explored. This would necessitate a knowledge of where to obtain access to these products and sometimes a minimum sum to invest. One often needs a minimum of $1,000 to $3,000 to buy into a life-cycle fund, for instance. Although life-cycle funds may indeed be a wonderful financial tool for many minimal-effort or minimal-knowledge investors, this minimum buy-in may well be out of reach.

In addition to access to the financial products of interest and the funds necessary to buy into some of these products, one would also need the confidence to make what might be very significant decisions in light of the overall value of one's financial portfolio. This is not the case for many individuals beginning their financial literacy journey. Although some demographics have been shown to generally overestimate their financial knowledge, others have been shown to systematically lack confidence; women, for instance, often rate their own financial knowledge lower than men, regardless of their actual level of knowledge.

Lastly, to be effective, personal financial literature requires that an individual has a definite and disciplined desire to learn about the topic at hand. Although there have been multiple examples of library programming incorporating financial literacy learning within other contexts—such as including the financial literacy components in ostensibly entertainment programming or through English as a Second Language (ESL) programs—personal finance texts tend to focus exclusively on financial literacy concepts. Although the tone of many of these books is intended to be engaging, they have little ostensible entertainment value and no social pressure to remain with the text. A reader must be fully intrinsically motivated.

A STATIC MEDIUM

Personal finance literature also has a number of downsides associated with the static nature of its medium. Financial guidance can grow outdated between editions, and this results in the potential for inaccurate information or unsound advice. In updating the financial recommendations in *Your Money or Your Life*, for example, Vicki Robin notes that Joe Dominguez, the book's original author, advocated fully investing in US Treasury bonds to ensure maximum safety of capital with virtually no risk to principal. In the years since his retirement in 1969, however, there have been instances where the yield on thirty-year US Treasury bonds has fallen below inflation. At these times, the advice to funnel all retirement investments into Treasury bonds would have resulted in a negative real yield.

All the advice within these covers also tends to be addressing the "average" audience. In order to sell copies, the advice needs to be perceived as applicable to the widest number of potential purchasers, and thus titles are not generally directed toward niche demographics. Instead, titles appeal as widely as possible to those who might potentially have the money to purchase the books; of the twelve books read for my previous article, for example, seven titles included the words *millionaire* or *rich*. General advice for the attainment of wealth, however, is not always the best financial advice, especially not for niche populations.

Lastly, the financial opinions conveyed within these texts often disagree with one another and have the potential to be misinterpreted by readers without the opportunity for the author to correct potentially harmful interpretations. The following are a few examples of potentially dangerous ideas:

- leveraging (borrowing money to buy assets, assuming you can pay back the loan when the assets appreciate)
- investing in a "focused" instead of a "balanced" way, a.k.a. *not* diversifying one's investment portfolio
- a "gazelle-intense" focus on debt repayment to the exclusion of even matched retirement contributions
- regularly using credit cards for living expenses while pursuing a desired career that doesn't offer a sufficient salary during the "dues-paying years"

Although none of this is necessarily bad advice given the particulars of one's individual situation, each recommendation certainly has the potential to cause a negative financial impact. Books, which are capable of providing only static, general advice, cannot clarify or counter any misperceptions.

AN IMPORTANT ROLE FOR LIBRARIES IN THE FINANCIAL LITERACY MOVEMENT

Libraries can fill—and I believe many *are* filling—much of the space popular personal finance literature leaves unattended. The Reference and

User Services Association (RUSA) document *Financial Literacy Education in Libraries: Guidelines and Best Practices for Service* takes pains to support the financial education of patrons who are in a variety of socioeconomic situations and who have potentially no background financial knowledge at all. Possible workshop topics suggested include the following:

- getting your first job
- what to do if your paycheck is not enough
- what to do if you lose your job
- when using credit is the right decision
- understanding payday and title loans
- how to select a bank
- understanding mutual funds[3]

These are only a few of the workshop topics posited, but they indicate an emphasis on addressing patrons who may face barriers to accessing popular personal finance texts, through either a lack of background knowledge or an inconsistent active income stream.

Libraries also frequently address more niche populations in their financial literacy programming. Smart investing@your library "model programs" include programs that target: women, youth, the elderly, families, and ESL immigrants and refugees, among others. These populations are arguably more at risk for financial instability, making these targeted programs a particularly important component to a community's overall financial health.

Library programming also has the advantage of being a dynamic as opposed to a static medium. Programs can be kept up to date with the latest information, and resources and programs can be adjusted as librarians get to know the needs of their particular patrons in increasing depth. The Central Library of Rochester and Monroe County, for instance, built its financial literacy programming with the assistance of an advisory panel from the local refugee population to help librarians "understand various community beliefs, gender roles, areas of misinformation, and cultural norms that impact financial behaviors."[4] No popular publication will ever be able to address that same level of specificity. Programs in libraries can also address basic literacy skills that may be hampering patrons' access to personal finance texts and especially basic computer literacy skills that are now frequently necessary in order to access certain financial products or opportunities. (Some job applications, for instance, are now available solely online or require an e-mail address as a contact point.)

Library programs can also bring in patrons who might not be fully intrinsically motivated to learn about financial literacy. When the Los Angeles Public Library surveyed their patrons, they found that "53% said they had never checked out library materials on financial matters, yet 77% said they would attend a finance-related workshop at the library."[5] This disparity could exist for any of a large number of reasons, but two particularly appealing aspects of programming versus educational texts may be that

1. programming is a smaller overall commitment of time and effort, and
2. programming sometimes can couch financial literacy education within other, potentially more appealing contexts.

Estes Valley Public Library in Ester Park, Colorado, for instance, used movie nights with titles like *Confessions of a Shopaholic* to spark mediated discussions on financial literacy topics. Providing patrons with the opportunity to explore financial literacy with a minimal investment of time and energy and the "accidental" learning that may occur when financial literacy concepts are incorporated into other types of library programs are advantages of a dynamic educational medium.

IDEAS LIBRARIES MIGHT BORROW FROM POPULAR PERSONAL FINANCE LITERATURE

With all this said regarding the things popular personal finance texts do *not* address, I want to make it a point to note that there are some very powerful and useful ideas within these texts that librarians might like to know about in order to enhance their own financial literacy or at least to be able to point patrons toward these texts when appropriate. Popular personal finance literature, for example, generally does a very good job of addressing the fact that there are emotional and behavioral aspects of money management. Although financial literacy would be infinitely simpler if we were all strictly rational creatures, the fact is that most peoples' financial choices are influenced by other factors. Dave Ramsey summarized it best when he wrote, "What to do isn't the problem; doing it is. Most of us know what to do, but we just don't do it. If I can control the guy in the mirror, I can be skinny and rich."[6] Although library programs may tend to focus on teaching people who honestly do *not* know what to do, the literature does do a good job of addressing various ways the people who know but don't do might better control their impulses.

One conceptualization of "money" within the literature is particularly impactful but not always discussed in traditional financial literacy programming: it is the idea that money is ultimately your life, your energy, your time. Most Americans make the majority of their earnings through "active income." We work a number of hours for a salary or wage. Thus we can think of money in terms of how many hours of our life it took to earn it. This has implications for how and why one might choose one career over another, the importance of negotiating one's salary at a new job, why one would spend more or less on the daily consumption of "small stuff," and/or why one might invest more or less heavily in obtaining the revered "passive income stream" for which one does *not* have to make a one-to-one trade of time for money. When one thinks of money in terms of one's *life*, it drives home how essential money management is to living the best possible life.

I also appreciate that personal finance literature is relentless in emphasizing the importance of steady investment and the idea that you must always "pay yourself first." I understand why library financial literacy programming, on a whole, has less emphasis on this concept, as it strikes one initially as another luxury issue, but the truth is investing is not a luxury in the long term. Although imminent financial survival may necessarily take up the majority of one's income stream, it is essential that if *at all possible*, something is invested at regular intervals in order to ensure *any* income stream in retirement. If one does not pay himself or herself first, chances are there's no money left over for investment at the end of each month. This is why so many Americans, even those who have sufficient steady income, have so little in retirement savings.

Lastly, understanding that retirement will necessitate a *stream* of income is a point popular personal finance literature is careful to distinguish. As George Clason explains so clearly in his 1955 book *The Richest Man in Babylon*, "A man's wealth is not the purse he carries. A fat purse quickly empties if there be no golden stream to refill it."[7] Many library patrons may imagine that saving for retirement or financial freedom involves achieving a static financial sum; it is important that the idea and importance of passive income be fully understood. Although the RUSA guidelines do mention possible workshop topics for investing and even "business income" related to "investment properties," the overarching concept that investing is a process through which one acquires assets that produce steady, passive income seems to be less emphasized in library financial literacy programming overall.[8]

WORKING HAND IN HAND

Ultimately, as is the general ideal of library collections and library programming working hand in hand, there is something to be said for the contributions of both popular personal finance literature and library financial literacy programming to the overall financial education of the population. I believe that library programming plays an essential role in addressing the financial literacy needs of those who require it the most. Library programming can serve as the very first step a patron takes in the pursuit of financial literacy; there are often no prerequisites. Libraries' programming can also serve as a more nuanced voice speaking directly to *their* particular patrons.

Popular personal finance books can serve as sources of more extensive learning in particular areas of interest. These books can feed the aspiration for financial freedom that should be the ultimate goal of every individual: a worry-free retirement. They can also allow patrons to explore multiple, divergent perspectives on any given issue and even allow them to explore less traditional financial advice and concepts. They can spark the conversations that continue at home after patrons have left the library.

Together, library programming and popular personal finance literature can certainly help people take their first few steps toward financial literacy and even financial stability. Although financial literacy is no guarantee of financial stability, research suggests it is certainly an important component. Hopefully, library programs and popular personal finance texts can help everyone achieve their "golden stream."

NOTES

1. Ashley E. Faulkner, "Financial Literacy Education in the United States: Exploring Popular Personal Finance Literature," *Journal of Librarianship and Information Science* 49, no. 3 (September 2017): 287–98. https://doi.org/10.1177/0961000615616106.

2. Federal Deposit Insurance Corporation, "2017 FDIC National Survey of Unbanked and Underbanked Households Executive Summary," October 2018, www.fdic.gov/house holdsurvey/2017/2017execsumm.pdf.

3. Reference and User Services Association, *Financial Literacy Education in Libraries: Guidelines and Best Practices for Service*, 2014, 3–5, 8–9, www.ala.org/rusa/sites/ala.org.rusa/files/content/FLEGuidelines_Final_September_2014.pdf.

4. Smart investing@your library, "Central Library of Rochester & Monroe County, Rochester, NY," https://smartinvesting.ala.org/central-library-of-rochester-monroe-county-rochester-ny/.

5. Smart investing@your library, "Los Angeles Public Library," https://smartinvesting.ala.org/los-angeles-public-library/.

6. Dave Ramsey, *The Total Money Makeover* (Nashville, TN: Thomas Nelson, 2009), 3.

7. George Clason, *The Richest Man in Babylon* (New York: Plume, 1955), 18.

8. Reference and User Services Association, *Financial Literacy Education,* 4.

Chapter 3

Financial Literacy Partners in the Community

BUSINESS COMMUNITY CONNECTIONS

◇◇◇◇◇◇◇◇◇◇◇◇◇◇◇◇◇◇◇◇◇◇◇◇◇◇◇◇◇◇◇◇◇◇◇◇◇◇◇

BARBARA A. ALVAREZ

Head of Adult Services

North Shore Library, Glendale, Wisconsin

P lanning library programs and events can be one of the most exciting aspects of librarianship. However, providing financial literacy programs is often met with hesitation and fear. And it is easy to understand why: financial literacy classes, workshops, and events at the library require a different planning process than traditional programming does.

Librarians are no doubt familiar with receiving cold calls from hopeful speakers, presenters, performers, and programmers who would like to partner with the library. Sometimes these individuals include financial advisors, investment bankers, and asset managers. In these cases, it is important for librarians to proceed with caution. Because of the sensitive nature of this topic, it is imperative that the presenters the library works with have the necessary credentials and qualifications to speak on the subject and are vetted by others. As librarians, there is the additional factor of ensuring that the presenters understand that these workshops and programs are not opportunities to sell services or products; they are strictly informational and/or instructional.

All these caveats can be enough to make any librarian shy away from providing financial literacy programs. And although this is understandable, those who ultimately are affected by this choice are the patrons who do not receive the free information and resources that can transform their relationship with money.

The most effective way to ensure a successful financial literacy event in coordination with the local business community is to develop connections with local business owners, entrepreneurs, financiers, and professionals so that they are well aware of the mission and goals of the library. Additionally, these connections will encourage the business community to have an equally vested interest in providing programs that serve the community, not just generate clients.

DO THE TWO-STEP

In order to secure high-quality presenters for financial literacy classes at the library, librarians will need to begin the work of scouting out potential partnerships well in advance in the *two-step process*. The two-step process focuses on networking and partnerships. The first step is to develop meaningful relationships in the business community. The second step is to utilize those relationships to build a financial literacy task force. For this to be successful, these steps must be done thoughtfully and strategically. Additionally, one cannot be done without the other. It may feel like a lot more work up front, but in the end, you will have an action plan and task force to carry you into planning financial literacy events for many years.

Step 1: Developing Meaningful Relationships

In order to provide library patrons with the best financial literacy workshops and classes, it is imperative to network outside of the library. This means that you will need to consistently leave the reference desk and meet the business community at their venues. This is called *embedded business librarianship*. Unlike outreach where the objective is to semiregularly go to community events or locations in order to promote the library, embedded business librarianship seeks to become *part* of the business community, attending business-related functions, events, and meetings.

But why does this matter to providing financial literacy programs? Because when someone is frequently making connections while representing the library, the anonymity of the library evaporates: people buy into the library's mission; there is human interest, and they want to be part of building a successful community. This means that not only will the business community be clear on who the library serves and what the library stands for, but the quality of the presentations and programs will increase because it will not be seen as an infomercial—there is now a personal connection.

The five parts to becoming embedded in your library's business community will take perseverance and may require you to leave your comfort zone. However, the rewards are worth it. In doing so, the library will not only learn about the unique culture, successes, and setbacks of the business community, but it will also develop relationships that are substantive and meaningful.

1. Assemble your list of businesses, organizations, and nonprofits that you would like to connect with for financial literacy events. This may include the Chamber of Commerce, merchant groups, small business development centers, community banks, nonprofit financial organizations, networking groups, entrepreneur forums, and educators at local schools or colleges. Meetup.com and Eventbrite.com are good websites to discover what type of events and groups are in your area.

2. After you have created and reviewed your list, choose one or two (to start!) that you would like to get to know better. Check out their website, subscribe to their e-mail list, and follow their social media to get a better idea of the type of work that they do and who they serve. When you are ready, you can reach out to someone at the organization or business via e-mail at first. This e-mail does not have to be lengthy—just a quick introduction of who you are and why you want to get to know more about them. Ask if there is an upcoming meeting or event that you can attend or if you can tour their location. Additionally, find out if they would be interested in you talking about a library-resource/business information topic at an upcoming meeting or event.

3. At the initial meeting, it is important that you enter with an open mind and a listening ear. Allow the business owner to share his or her history, purpose, triumphs, and struggles without judgment or knee-jerk solutions. This will be more impactful than handing out a bunch of library brochures that may or may not be relevant to the business owner's needs. If you do discuss library resources, talk about the lesser-known services, like conference rooms, technology

assistance, relevant databases, and instructional classes. You can also share library challenges, like reaching millennials or those with limited transportation. By showing that the library has no other agenda but to listen and develop a relationship, the business community will be more receptive to continuing partnerships.

4. At the conclusion of your meeting, leave a business card and a call to action, such as an invitation to an upcoming library event, a group training on social media or something similar, or just a future coffee date. Whichever you decide, it is imperative that when you leave that initial meeting, you have created an incentive to meet within the next two to three weeks. This will establish ongoing communication and differentiate your relationship from a standard outreach experience.

5. Continue to network in the business community by attending meetings, events, ribbon cuttings, open houses, career fairs, networking scrambles, and so on. The key is consistency: meet, network, repeat. The more that you keep your face in the community, the more the library will develop a reputation as being *part* of the business community, not a separate entity.

When the library has that personal connection with the business community, the status of the library is elevated because business owners, professionals, and entrepreneurs feel heard, recognized, and supported. Additionally, they will learn more about the functions of the library on a more meaningful level, deepening their understanding of the library's mission and goals. Ultimately, the objective is to change the mind-set of "It's strange that the library is involved in the business community" to "It would be strange if the library *weren't* involved in the business community."

Step 2: Building a Task Force

You may be wondering how you can transition these interactions to financial literacy programs at the library. As we move into the second phase of preparing for financial literacy workshops and programs at the library, the time you took developing relationships will have been well spent. The next component is to invite individuals who you feel would be good stewards for financial literacy events to a library-led financial literacy task force.

There are many benefits to having a financial literacy task force instead of hiring presenters and instructors in insolation. To begin with, the task force creates a sense of unity between the different participants with the library at the focal point. Second, task force members will be clear on why financial literacy programs at the library are important. Additionally, participants will understand that financial literacy workshops should be informational, not commercial, and they will have a team of peers to hold them accountable.

There is flexibility in how the task force can operate. Some of the variables include the following:

- whether this is an ongoing task force or specifically for the annual Money Smart Week
- how many members will be part of it
- the inclusion (or exclusion) of different financial resources, organizations, and businesses in the area
- whether task force members should recruit speakers or present themselves
- if presentations and instructional material should be submitted for approval to the task force before the event at the library
- if there should be a social media strategy as well as a recruitment of businesses and organizations to cross-promote the event for community-wide awareness
- what the end goal of the financial literacy event is

How you determine the task force should function is your choice. The most important aspect of the task force is that people are more invested when they feel that they are serving a bigger purpose than simply "speaking at the library."

While you continue to embed yourself in the business community, you can start to build your task force and present information about hosting financial literacy workshops and events at the library. At this point, your relationships should be at a level where you feel comfortable asking to speak at an upcoming meeting, publish a guest post in the next e-newsletter, or present at a future Chamber of Commerce gathering. Alternatively, you may elect to meet with individuals one-on-one. Regardless of how you decide to approach this, it is important that you utilize visuals and stories to convey passion and need for financial literacy at the library. These presentations should invigorate and inspire the business community by advocating for a holistic initiative that improves the financial well-being of the community. The following are some suggestions:

- **Length:** Remember that a short but powerful presentation goes further than a long, dense speech.
- **Statistics:** Provide statistics for unemployment, bankruptcy, college debt, and lack of retirement funds—numbers are important in demonstrating urgency. Take a look at your own statistics at the library as well as any information that local organizations may be able to share. Check out the United States Census Bureau (https://census.gov) and Pew Research Center (www.pewresearch.org) for state and national statistics.
- **Stories:** Do you have a story that you can share (with permission or omitting recognizable information) about the need for financial literacy or how the library has made a positive impact?
- **Infographics:** Combine the information into a visually appealing display. Check out canva.com or piktochart.com for free Infographic makers.
- **Media:** Consider how short video clips, social media livestreams, press releases, and collaborations with local radio or TV programs could boost your message in recruiting task force members and promoting financial literacy at the library.

Because of your networking in step 1, the business community knows your library and its core values. This means that recruiting individuals will no longer be a transactional relationship. Instead, it will be an interactional relationship. So instead of selecting someone who really doesn't understand the library, its patrons, and the purpose of financial literacy at the library, you will recruit individuals to the task force who share a mutual goal with the library.

ALA Editions editor Patrick Hogan interviewed Terry Ratoff, the business services librarian at Skokie (Illinois) Public Library, to learn about partnering with local businesses and organizations for business and financial literacy programming. She is part of a community engagement team that includes staff offering services related to youth, people with disabilities, seniors, and immigrants and includes a bookmobile. Holding a master of business administration from the University of North Carolina at Chapel Hill, Terry worked in business before pursuing librarianship and getting her master of library science.

Terry actively networks with community partners, such as the Skokie Chamber of Commerce, and meets with local business owners and aspiring entrepreneurs. She attends Skokie's Economic Development Commission meetings and site visits and contributes to special task forces when invited. She also networks with a group of business librarians from local public libraries. They meet quarterly to compare notes on their programs, recommend presenters, and learn from professional speakers on a variety of business topics.

Another opportunity to connect is through the library's services to local businesses. The library makes meeting rooms available to local businesses for their events and meetings. Nonresident employees of businesses in the village and members of the Skokie Chamber of Commerce can obtain business library cards to use library meeting rooms and resources. In partnership with SCORE volunteers, the library offers free counseling to businesses and nonprofits on issues such as financing, marketing, and writing business plans.

As Terry gets to know the business people in the community, they get to know the library. It helps when she is looking for presenters. Terry attends external presentations whenever possible. That way, she sees the presenters she wants to invite back or refer to her peers at neighboring libraries. Terry is not concerned about pitches from presenters she knows. "They understand what the library does and what our goals are," she said. If a sales pitch does break out, she can politely redirect.

The library offers five to eight financial literacy programs annually, including three to four during Money Smart Week. For example, a representative of a local bank presented the program "How to Stop Being Broke." Though knowledgeable staff will present occasionally on a topic such as budgeting with Excel, the library often engages outside presenters. Congresswoman Jan Schakowsky's office referred a presenter to speak about Social Security. A State of Illinois staff member helped people locate unclaimed funds through their "iCash" program. A project manager with the Fair Lending/ Home Preservation Law Project at the John Marshall Law School in Chicago presented on Housing and Urban Development–approved reverse mortgages. "Credit unions are also a good source for presenters because they have an educational mission, like the library," she said. Credit unions have presented at the library about auto loans and rent-or-buy housing decisions.

Because the library focuses on being community driven, others recognize it as being a key contributor to community economic development.

CONCLUSION

Financial literacy program planning can feel like a daunting endeavor. This largely comes from the disconnect between the business community and the library: instead of the library being seen as part of the local community, it is often seen as a separate entity with little to no identity. However, when the business community and the library interact in the same spheres, these barriers begin to collapse. Financial literacy initiatives are opportune to further progressing those connections through partnerships and a common goal. In following the two-step process of developing meaningful relationships and building a financial literacy task force, the foundational work of improving the quality of life in the community is achieved.

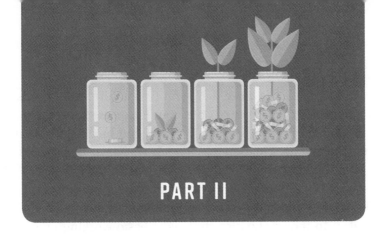

PART II

The Programs

GETTING STARTED IN FINANCIAL LITERACY PROGRAMMING

As librarians and library staff, you are keenly aware of the critical role that programming plays in library service. Programming allows for the exploration of ideas in an informal, comfortable setting, allowing learners of all ages to engage their different learning styles on a variety of topics. Programs also foster social connections and reinforce the notion of the library as a center for lifelong learning, as a place to not just exercise intellect but also develop life skills—as a helper.

So why is it important for the library to offer programs on financial literacy topics? First, library-goers prefer to learn about finance topics in person. According to ALA's *Report of the 2016 Public Library Personal Finance Survey*, public library patrons "most commonly receive personal finance information in the form of programs, commonly in the workshop, seminar or speaker format."[1] Some popular topics that public library patrons are learning about include retirement planning, consumer protection and fraud, financing college, and investing.

The second reason is more democratic in nature. The results of the Federal Reserve's 2016 Survey of Consumer Finances show that "financial literacy is strongly linked to education level and income. This pattern is worrisome because poor households not only earn less but also tend to lack the financial knowledge needed to manage their income properly."[2] Given libraries' broad community reach, financial literacy programs in libraries can make up that gap and provide additional learning and skill-building opportunities to those who already have a basic working knowledge of personal finance concepts. High-quality, engaging library programs are an important way to increase financial literacy in your community.

Different learners will have different needs. College students may be interested in programs that include strategies for managing student loan debt. Preschoolers will benefit from programs that introduce the concept of money and what we do with it. Middle schoolers are starting to think about their future and how to achieve their goals. Retirees may want to know more about making the best of their retirement savings and avoiding fraud. New immigrants are learning US financial systems. Parents may be uncomfortable discussing money with their children—intergenerational programming allows both parents and kids to learn about personal finance topics in a comfortable environment.

As with everything in the library, knowing the needs and interests of your community is key. Discussing these needs and interests with your patrons and community partners and learning from national studies such as the FINRA Investor Education Foundation's *National Financial Capability Study* can help you prioritize topics to focus on.[3]

You'll see that you are not alone when planning financial literacy programming. You can choose to run something yourself if your personal knowledge and library staff capacity allow for it. However, this topic easily lends itself to partnerships with community-based organizations and experts. Qualified, nonbiased partners and presenters such as credit unions, universities and community colleges, extension services, community organizations, government agencies, and schools are assets to your program planning and implementation.

Many libraries incorporate financial literacy programs into annual initiatives such as Money Smart Week or National Library Week. Others utilize special opportunities such as hosting a financial literacy traveling exhibition or applying for—and receiving—a grant to prioritize personal finance into a theme for the year; others find ways to fold finance concepts into interdisciplinary learning, where financial literacy is just one of several goals of the program. Some programs are brand new to the library, while others are repackaged from previous programs or existing in-house resources.

Perhaps you already have experience with programming in general. Or maybe you have expertise in business or personal finance reference but less so in programming. Maybe you're concerned about your own personal finance knowledge and not sure where to begin. What follows are examples of programs implemented in several library types, for various age groups, in communities large and small across the United States. Whether you already implement personal finance programs or have never done anything on the topic, we hope the following program models will provide inspiration and frameworks to try out something new.

NOTES

1. K. Henke, *Report of the 2016 Public Library Personal Finance Survey* (Chicago: ALA, 2017).
2. YiLi Chien, "How Do Americans Rate in Financial Literacy?," Federal Reserve Bank of St. Louis, *St. Louis Fed on the Economy* (blog), September 18, 2018, www.stlouisfed.org/on-the-economy/2018/september/how-americans-rate-financial-literacy.
3. Since 2009, FINRA Investor Education Foundation has commissioned a national study every few years that looks at the financial capability of U.S. adults. For the most recent study, see Judy T. Lin, Christopher Bumcrot, Tippy Ulicny, Gary Mottola, Gerri Walsh, Robert Ganem, Christine Kieffer, and Annamaria Lusardi, *The State of U.S. Financial Capability: The 2018 National Financial Capability Study* (Washington, DC: Finra Investor Education Foundation, 2019), https://www.usfinancialcapability.org/downloads/NFCS_2018_Report_Natl_Findings.pdf.

Chapter 4

Art Shop

IGNITING FAMILY FINANCIAL CONVERSATIONS

◇◇◇◇◇◇◇◇◇◇◇◇◇◇◇◇◇◇◇◇◇◇◇◇◇◇◇◇◇◇◇◇

CECILY PONCE DE LEON
Programming Manager
Plano Public Library, Plano, Texas

LIBRARY TYPE	Public library

ABOUT THE LIBRARY

Plano is a young, ethnically diverse suburban community of 285,000 located about twenty miles north of Dallas. The median age of Plano residents is thirty-seven, and the city is home to nearly 56,000 Asian American and 42,000 Hispanic residents. Approximately three in ten Plano residents speak a language other than English at home, and nearly a quarter were born outside the United States, representing twenty-six nationalities. Plano Public Library has a unique opportunity to serve as a link to acculturation and learning and reaches its constituents through five library locations.

ABOUT THE PROGRAM

Art Shop is a hands-on program for families that promotes financial literacy, decision-making, resourcefulness, and creativity. In this sixty-minute program combining budgeting, process art, and project design, kids are invited to answer the question, "What can you create with five dollars?" Provided with a "wallet" containing five dollars in play money, participants browse the "art shop" for supplies to make their own masterpieces.

Creativity abounds, but the key is the opportunity for children to gain experience planning, making choices, "purchasing" supplies, and working within a budget. Participation provides parents with tools for facilitating conversations around finances outside the library.

TARGET AUDIENCE	Kids (ages 3–7), tweens (ages 8–12), and their families
PROGRAM BUDGET	$101–$250

The goals of this program include the following:

- Facilitate family engagement around the concept of budgeting and spending; the activity is for children, but we strongly encourage parent participation to begin conversations about budgeting, planning, and goal setting that may extend beyond the library program.
- Engage children within a safe space to learn about spending power— to help children learn through exploration (purchases, returns, wise use of resources, pooling resources).
- Allow children to practice basic budgeting and use basic math skills with purchasing transactions.
- Connect the financial literacy elements to STEAM (art) programming, which is a priority in programming for children and families.

Planning begins about one month in advance of the program to collect and organize supplies, assemble the "wallets," and create signage and price tags to create the "shop." Preparations can easily be managed by one to two staff members, and the event can be scaled to be presented by anywhere from two to six facilitators. Art Shop is simple enough that it could be managed easily by one staff person along with community volunteers. It is a straightforward and easily reproducible program that can use any art or craft materials you may have on hand, and it does not require any special equipment.

This particular program did not require partners. However, there is potential to involve community volunteers as partners to run the "store," distribute the wallets as participants enter, and photograph or display completed artwork.

We use the following materials and supplies:

- wallets
  - Ziploc bag or envelope to hold the play money
  - shipping labels to list contents of wallets
  - play money, total of five dollars in each wallet (three one-dollar bills, five quarters, five dimes, and five nickels); printed paper money and coins work too
- poster board to create Art Shop supply and price list
  - art supplies/merchandise: anything you have on hand or that is easily collected, including construction paper, paper bags, stickers, feathers, paint, ribbon, craft foam, coffee filters, paper plates, fabric scraps, buttons, pom-poms, glue, glitter, popsicle sticks, and pipe cleaners
- cash register: a cardboard box or any other item to organize the play money; should be stocked with some additional play money to make change for participants
- *optional*
  - program tickets if necessary to limit attendance
  - butcher paper or other disposable materials to cover work surfaces and protect from glue, paint, and so on
  - trays, plates, or baskets for participants to carry "purchased" items to their workstations

The costs associated with this program are for art materials, play money, and supplies to create a "shop." The estimate for cost is made with the assumption that you will need to purchase all art supplies and play money, but this is a generous estimate and can vary widely. Donated or previously purchased art materials may be used. If your budget is limited, you can be creative with items "sold" in the art shop or seek donations to supply the program.

The event is promoted via the regular means of the library, including library program brochures (twenty-four-page full-color publications printed seasonally, three times per year), the library website, posters posted in each of the five library locations, the digital newsletter *Check It Out!*, a library blog, local print media, and social media.

This program can be set up according to building space. It is recommended that you have the following:

- material stations—the "store"
    - up to three tables organized by material type
    - labeled art supplies and assigned prices
- creation stations
    - multiple tables or workspaces for participants to create their art projects
    - *optional*: cover the creation stations with butcher paper or another disposable material to protect the surface from spills and messes
    - *optional*: lunch trays, paper plates, or baskets for participants to carry supplies from the "store" and facilitate easy cleanup

Plano Public Library sets up three "vendor" stations with craft materials for purchase, with a staff member or volunteer acting as the cashier for transactions at each station.

We offer Art Shop as a ticketed event, meaning attendance is limited by the number of wallets prepared in advance. The program admits a maximum of fifty children, plus parents. Free tickets are distributed starting thirty minutes in advance of the program.

As families enter the room, they are given a wallet and orientation to the Art Shop, including the rules for conduct, purchase, and returns. Facilitators encourage kids to spend a few minutes budgeting the supplies they want to purchase and to think about what kind of art they want to create, but participants are allowed to begin making purchases immediately.

Once they've begun, participants need very little guidance. The lead staff member circulates through the room to answer questions. Facilitators prompt participants throughout the program to consider how they are spending their money and to think creatively about how they could meet their goals and make their art projects. No guidelines are given on what they are to create. Children are encouraged to consider pooling their resources to purchase what they need and to think about sharing items with others. Siblings in attendance do this often.

The program carries a "return policy," which allows participants to return unused items and have their money refunded to purchase additional items. No returns are given for partially used items (e.g., paper that has been cut).

At the end of the program, surveys are distributed for the parents to fill out and are collected at the door as participants exit. Parents have given positive comments and are extremely enthusiastic about giving their children practical examples of how to use money for purchasing items.

OPTIONAL ACTIVITIES AND ADJUSTMENTS TO CONSIDER

- **Preprogram lesson for kids:** Before the "shop" opens, walk participants through a basic budgeting lesson. We encourage parent participation to facilitate these conversations, but you could also present this as a kids-only program and provide instruction and budgeting sheets to the participants.
- **Older tweens or teens:** You could include the budgeting and financial literacy elements as part of a larger design challenge program where participants are tasked with purchasing supplies to solve a problem or provide a solution to a real-life issue (e.g., build the tallest structure or design an object that would solve an everyday problem like losing your keys). This would replace the process art project.

Art Shop has been offered as a sixty-minute program, but the length of the program can be adjusted depending on your needs. We find that children need extra time to complete their art projects after taking time to plan, budget, and purchase supplies. Another option is to offer the program in a two-hour, come-and-go format. Once a participant leaves, their wallet could be refilled with play money and given to a new participant. It is helpful for staff to remain aware of the time left in the program to give cleanup reminders.

Plano Public Library has welcomed between forty and fifty attendees at each event. Parents have given overwhelmingly positive feedback and expressed gratitude for the opportunity for their children to learn skills such as planning, budgeting, making changes, pooling and stretching resources, making a return, and being responsible for funds. Many parents are surprised and impressed with what their children are able to accomplish, though they had not previously thought to begin conversations at home around money management. With Art Shop, we are meeting our program objective of starting family conversations around financial literacy concepts with our youngest members.

In all our financial literacy programming, the biggest revelation for staff has been the ease of incorporating basic financial concepts into existing programs for children and families. We challenge you to think about ways to incorporate simple lessons and exercises on budgeting, saving, spending, planning for the future, and more into existing programs for your youngest library customers.

Chapter 5

Money Smart Week at Your Tribal Library

◇◇◇◇◇◇◇◇◇◇◇◇◇◇◇◇◇◇◇◇◇◇◇◇◇◇◇◇◇◇◇◇◇◇◇◇◇◇

ANNE HEIDEMANN
Tribal Librarian
Saginaw Chippewa Tribal Library, Mount Pleasant, Michigan

LIBRARY TYPE	Public and tribal library

ABOUT THE LIBRARY

The Saginaw Chippewa Tribal Library is a public library operated by the Saginaw Chippewa Indian Tribe of Michigan, a federally recognized Indian tribe established by treaty on August 2, 1855. Open to all, this library serves the community, including tribal members and descendants, employees of the tribe, and others, and is staffed, together with Saginaw Chippewa Tribal College Library and Saginaw Chippewa Academy (elementary school) library, by one librarian and two library assistants. The tribal library is a typical small rural public library, which also strives to incorporate Anishinaabe culture and language into all aspects of service.

ABOUT THE PROGRAM

Money Smart Week at Saginaw Chippewa Tribal Library is an annual program featuring a storytime-style interactive read-aloud, zhoonya (money) game in Anishinaabemowin, and take-homes from the library, the language revitalization department, and the local credit union.

TARGET AUDIENCE	All ages
PROGRAM BUDGET	Free

Money Smart Week is one of the annual events that Saginaw Chippewa Tribal Libraries have become known for in the community in recent years. Starting in 2014 and taking place every year since, the tribal libraries celebrate Money Smart Week through a storytime event for families and through a variety of promotions that community members can take advantage of at their leisure. When we started planning our first Money Smart Week, we wanted to provide a program that promoted financial literacy, brought attention to the libraries' resources related to financial matters, and supported the ongoing community-wide effort to promote fluency in Anishinaabemowin. The Money Smart Week plan we came up with consists of one in-person storytime event, which is open to all ages but is particularly promoted to families and is supplemented by promotional efforts and passive programs of interest to other target audiences. We try to make the whole week a celebration of financial literacy, observed in a variety of ways.

We chose to hold our in-person storytime event at the tribal (public) library because it is open to everyone and is centrally located in the tribal operations building, convenient and nearby to many other gathering places on the reservation. We promote the storytime event at our other two locations but do not hold in-person events at those sites. Because our three staff members are typically spread out covering three library locations, it is highly beneficial for us to have a program that is relatively low maintenance and requires the presence of only one library staff member. Working with community partners has allowed us to meet all our goals for this program while still staffing all our locations. While our partners deliver the program content, the library staff member provides introductions, takes photos, manages the giveaway items, and ensures that things run smoothly throughout while still being able to assist other patrons if needed. The tribal library is quite limited in space, so we host programs like this in the children's area of the library (rather than in a dedicated, separate room, as it might be in a larger library). The library service desk is located in the children's half of the library, which means that it is feasible for one person to manage both a program and the desk at the same time. As the children's half of the library can accommodate only seventeen people at a time, per the fire code, we limit registration to around a dozen attendees. Typically we will have several families attend, some of whom bring along cousins, neighbors, or other friends.

Our Money Smart Week celebration has evolved each year, but the storytime generally consists of a read-aloud of that year's official Money Smart Week picture book followed by a zhoonya (money) game in which participants learn and practice the names for denominations of zhoonya in Anishinaabemowin. For this event, we reached out to a local credit union, which generously offered the services of one of their representatives to read at the storytime and provided giveaway items that promote personal saving to kids, usually a piggy bank with a voucher for a free savings account prestocked with five dollars. The credit union representative also incorporates interactive discussion about financial literacy concepts appropriate to the ages of the attendees. Outreach staff from the tribe's Anishinaabe Language Revitalization Department created the zhoonya game, which they present at the storytime event. This game provides not only Anishinaabemowin instruction and practice; it also incorporates math and financial literacy concepts. Attendees receive a copy of the official Money Smart Week picture book for that year (provided free to the library through registration on the Money Smart Week website) to add to their home libraries. The library also provides other items such as bookmarks, which we create in-house.

In addition to the in-person event, the libraries also promote Money Smart Week via community networks, social media, and displays. Target audiences we try to reach through these efforts have included elders, college students, tribal employees, teens, and new adults. Through past collection-focused grants, we have built robust collections of materials related to financial topics at each of the three library sites. During Money Smart Week, we create displays of these materials and circulate annotated lists of recommended titles through bibliography bookmarks, online, and via community networks. We utilize resources from the official Money Smart Week website and the CFPB to create our bookmarks and to offer free fact sheets, brochures, and other guides that community members can take home with them. One way we have gotten tribal employees involved is by sending out daily financial-themed trivia questions using the tribal operations network and rewarding winners with small prizes, such as novelty bags of shredded currency (provided to the library for free by Money Smart Week). We have also hosted Money Smart Week Open House Hours during which community members are welcomed to the tribal library to peruse our displays, help themselves to freebies, and share their own tips for being money-smart with other attendees. Representatives from other tribal departments, including the planning and the housing authority, have attended both to find out more about the library's new resources and to share information about their financial-related services. These open house hours allow for a steady flow of community members over time but never so many at once that it becomes overwhelming or overcrowded.

Because of ever-present budget constraints, we rely on the generosity of community partners and official initiatives like Money Smart Week so this program can happen without any dedicated financial outlay from the library's tribal funding. Our Money Smart Week requires only time from staff and our community partners, and the minimal costs of paper and printer toner for bookmarks and such are covered by the library's general supply. We create the promotional materials in-house using the official Money Smart Week graphics and with the assistance of staff from the tribal public relations office.

We have received feedback consistently over the years that indicates that community members value Money Smart Week and look forward to it each year. We generally have a full house for the storytime event, and the entire program is one that community members have repeatedly mentioned on general satisfaction surveys at other times of the year. Comments from staff, community partners, and attendees note that they love to see and experience the interaction between the presenters and the kids and that they feel that financial literacy is an important topic for all ages. Tribal libraries staff are pleased that the tribal libraries are able to provide a robust range of programs dedicated to financial literacy through Money Smart Week at Your Tribal Library.

Chapter 6

Family Sleepover at the Library

DOLLARS AND SENSE EDITION

◇◇

SUSAN CLAUS

Manager, Children's and Teen Services
Northland Public Library, Pittsburgh, Pennsylvania

LIBRARY TYPE	Public library

ABOUT THE LIBRARY

Northland is a suburban library just north of Pittsburgh in Allegheny County. We are an authority supported by five municipalities, serving 29,323 active cardholders from a service-area population of approximately 81,000. Families move to this area because of the strong schools. Northland's children and teens' service department has a staff of eight: two full-time librarians, four part-time librarians, and two full-time library assistants. All of our in-library and outreach programming is done from a single location. Northland is an independent library, but we are a member of a countywide consortium. We all share a union catalog, and materials at all libraries can be reserved and sent to any other library in the county.

ABOUT THE PROGRAM

Family Sleepover at the Library: Dollars and Sense edition is a financial literacy–themed after-hours program for families with children in kindergarten through fifth grade.

TARGET AUDIENCE	Families with children ages 5–11
PROGRAM BUDGET	$101–$250

Because most parents would rather have a root canal than talk about financial matters with their children, we did not announce the theme of the sleepover ahead of time. We marketed the overnight program as a chance to enjoy a storyteller, a craft, games, sleeping in the stacks, and breakfast in the morning, without divulging the theme.

We marketed the sleepover in our newsletter, in neighborhood magazines, on our website, and through social media. We charged a nominal fee of five dollars per person to cover some of the cost of craft materials, prizes, and a substantial continental breakfast spread. Families registered each person separately online. Even with the fee, we maxed out our registration at thirty, wanting to keep the numbers manageable.

The sleepover requires a tag team of two staff members to make splitting the group into two for games and crafts easier. A third person to take care of the unexpected is useful but not always possible due to staff schedules.

We started planning in January to meet the deadlines for neighborhood magazines. We sent the information to our marketing department six weeks ahead of time to give them time to design and produce print posters, quarter-sheet flyers, and digital graphics for social media.

A month ahead, we kicked around ideas, booked the professional storyteller, and searched Pinterest for minute-to-win-it games with money themes. About the same time, we ordered paint-it-yourself owl-shaped piggybanks online and "Money as You Grow" bookshelf pamphlets from the federal government's CFPB. Northland shares a catalog and materials with other libraries in the county, so we were able to have multiple copies of the books from the "Money as You Grow" bookshelf on hand for families to read or check out. In addition, we put out books on financial planning for the parents.

The week before the sleepover, we assembled what we needed for the games and prepped the parcel for the Pass the Parcel game. (See details later.) We had done research on what financial literacy for young children looks like using the Pennsylvania Department of Education state standards, so our modest financial literacy goals for the evening were highlighting saving versus spending and recognizing coins and currency.

On Friday nights, Northland closes at 6 p.m., and families arrived a half hour after closing. Families spread out through the children's room, staked out spots for sleeping bags, and assembled for snacks and self-directed games while waiting for everyone to arrive. We had filled a mason jar with loose change and invited the kids to guess how much money was in the jar. They wrote their guesses on slips of paper, with the winner to be announced at breakfast. The closest correct guess won all the money in the jar. There were also financial word-search puzzles to work on, just for fun.

Once we had everyone, our storyteller led a lively half hour of stories. She presented a selection of folktales about hard work rewarded, greed punished, and treasures found by those worthy of it. After storytime, we divided the families into two groups and led half to the tables set up for crafts and half to the room where the minute-to-win-it games were waiting.

We put out bisque owl banks from Oriental Trading along with smocks, paintbrushes, and sparkly acrylic paint. We had the kids write their names on sturdy paper plates and put the owl banks on the plates before painting. We knew the owls would not dry fully until breakfast, so the plates made them easy to move out of the way to a book cart to dry. Gloss paint gave them a nice, finished look.

We put out a make-and-take coin matching game, and kids who finished painting their owls with time to spare could make and play the matching game. Kids who took the whole hour to paint took their matching game home to make later.

While half the families were painting banks, other families were down the hall taking turns going through the minute-to-win-it course. The games were a combination of skill and luck. Each leg of the course had to be done by a single family member, so families strategized about who would be best for each game. The games had to be done in order, and each game had to be completed before the next was started. The librarian gave the "go" signal and started the stopwatch as the first player dove into the first game.

- **Game one:** Money Run. Players had to complete a slalom course that had to be done "crab-walk" style. Five traffic cones were decorated with large cutouts of coins and placed about five feet apart.

As soon as the crab walker cleared the last traffic cone, the next family member raced to start the milk-bottle game.

- **Game two:** Milk-Bottle Drop. Players had twenty pennies that had to be dropped from a standing position into a glass milk bottle. (The Whole Foods in my area still sells pints of milk in glass bottles, if you don't happen to have one handy.)
- **Game three:** Dollar-Bill Puzzle. We had drawn a dollar bill onto green poster board with a broad marker and cut it into random shapes, which were scattered on the ground. (We thought this would be the easiest game, but the puzzle proved surprisingly hard to reassemble!)
- **Game four:** Famous Founders. Three green latex balloons with the names of the founding fathers found on paper currency (in this case, Washington, Jefferson, and Franklin) had to be stuck to the wall using static electricity generated by rubbing the balloon on the player's hair.
- **Game five:** Money in the Bank. The "bank" was a masking-tape rectangle approximately twelve inches by fifteen inches. Players used a piece of cardboard to fan a dollar bill into the bank from a masking-tape starting line ten feet away.

As each family ran the course, their time was clocked on a stopwatch. We recorded the time it took them to finish the course and then subtracted as many seconds from their time as they had managed to put pennies in the milk bottle (e.g., four minutes and twelve seconds minus six pennies for a total time of four minutes and six seconds). We kept the results secret in order to announce the top three families and award their prizes at breakfast.

It took only a minute or two for staff to reset the course for the next contestants. Those who had already run it or were waiting their turn cheered on the others from the sidelines.

The two groups swapped places, gamers painting owls and crafters running the minute-to-win-it course. When both groups were done, families changed into their pajamas and came back together for one last game: Pass the Parcel.

Pass the Parcel has an element of risk versus reward and has to be prepared ahead of time. A grand prize (in this case, a small cardboard box with five Sacajawea one-dollar coins) is wrapped up in gift paper, and then forty more layers are wrapped around it. Randomly, these layers hold a small prize (like the foreign coins that seem to end up in our cash register) or a layer of nothing or a layer with a "forfeit" ("Bark like a dog," "Stand up and sing 'Twinkle, Twinkle Little Star' like an opera singer"). Players sit in a circle on the floor and pass the parcel from player to player. Each player must decide whether to unwrap one layer or pass it on without unwrapping to avoid risking having to do an embarrassing forfeit. The player to unwrap the last layer is the winner and keeps the prize.

After a bedtime snack of popcorn, milk, and hot chocolate, the families settled into their sleeping bags in the stacks to read by flashlight until lights out at 11:30 p.m.

The librarians were up by 5 a.m. to set out the fruit, bagels, cream cheese, cereal, milk, mini muffins, tea, and coffee. We announced the winners of the guessing game and the minute-to-win-it games, reunited the dry owl banks with their owners, and sent the families out, so the children's department could be cleaned up and reset before opening. Next time, we will ask our local banks and credit unions as well as the Modern Woodmen of America for swag to give the families.

Chapter 7

Play and Learn Career Center

◇◇

SUSAN CLAUS

Manager, Children's and Teen Services

Northland Public Library, Pittsburgh, Pennsylvania

LIBRARY TYPE	Public library

ABOUT THE LIBRARY

Northland is a suburban library just north of Pittsburgh in Allegheny County. We are an authority supported by five municipalities, serving 29,323 active cardholders from a service-area population of approximately 81,000. Families move to this area because of the strong schools. Northland's children and teens' service department has a staff of eight: two full-time librarians, four part-time librarians, and two full-time library assistants. All of our in-library and outreach programming is done from a single location. Northland is an independent library, but we are a member of a countywide consortium. We all share a union catalog, and materials at all libraries can be reserved and sent to any other library in the county.

ABOUT THE PROGRAM

Play and Learn Career Center is a self-directed dramatic-play activity area to introduce toddlers and preschoolers to economic concepts in line with the Pennsylvania standards for early childhood education.

TARGET AUDIENCE	Toddlers through five-year-olds
PROGRAM BUDGET	$251–$500 initial investment

Staff from our library took the training to become a Family Place library[1] early in 2010, and later that year, we converted our program room (which had been long outgrown for storytime crowds) into a Playful Parenting Room—a place for families with babies through five-year-olds to read and play together with developmentally appropriate materials. Family Place training encourages dramatic play with kitchen toys and dolls, and we knew that we wanted to expand this to include career clothes and a play stand that could become a grocery store, book store, veterinarian's office, and so on.

We based our goals for learning in our career center on the Pennsylvania Department of Human Services/Department of Education standards for early childhood education in economics, specifically the sections that have to do with the concepts and competencies involved in helping learners accomplish the following:

- know that to buy things, you need money
- understand that adults work at different jobs to earn money
- use play money to buy pretend goods and services
- role-play careers they see around them (grocery stores, pet stores, community helpers, etc.)

All these play activities take place in a self-directed and open-ended way. The atmosphere of the Playful Parenting Room encourages interaction between grown-ups and children, and we hope that the play around career toys, clothes, and props open up a space for dialogue about spending and saving. In addition, there is a bookshelf with books for parents and caregivers that includes materials on family financial planning and how to talk with children about finances.

In addition to the financial literacy component, there are additional benefits of social and emotional learning (that come as the career play lends itself to children drawing other children into the pretend world of their stores and careers) and growth in vocabulary.

The list of materials we put together for career play includes the following:

- market stand that has a chalkboard sign, countertop, and shelves that can be turned into many different businesses
- toy groceries (canned goods, vegetables, etc.)
- police uniform
- mail-carrier uniform
- chef clothes
- firefighter uniform
- construction worker vest and hardhat
- tools and tool belt
- doctor/veterinarian scrubs
- lab coat
- kitchen setup
- small table and chairs

We marketed the opening of our Family Place area with lots of fanfare in the local papers, in our newsletter, and through posters and flyers. The room quickly became a destination for families with young children, and now new families find us, having heard about the Playful Parenting Room from friends and neighbors (as well as through occasional mentions in the library guinea pig's Facebook posts).

We received a grant to start up our Family Place area and pursued a separate grant from the Northland Library Foundation to purchase the play stand and career clothes, toys, and props. The initial amount spent was just under $400. Each year, some of the clothes, toys, and props need to be replaced (our young entrepreneurs are especially hard on cash registers), so we expect to spend between fifty dollars and one hundred dollars on replacement materials and on new things to add interest to the collection. Some new career items have come as in-kind gifts through a kindergarten readiness program from the Pennsylvania Department of Commonwealth Libraries.

The day-to-day maintenance of the career area of the Playful Parenting Room varies. We reset the toys and props each morning, and depending on the tidiness of the grown-ups who have brought their children to play in the room the day before, it can take anywhere from five minutes to a half hour to get everything put in order. About once a month, we rotate the career clothes so they can be laundered and "new" career clothes and props put out to keep interest fresh. Sometimes at the start of the day, we stage the play stand as a bookstore or post office, but it tends to revert to a grocery store by closing time.

Several hundred children and families visit our Playful Parenting Room each week, and based on observation, most of the children ages three through five spend at least some of their time engaged in career play during their visit.

The financial outlay for career toys and props pays off in open-ended, self-directed play that invites young children to explore the adult world of careers. Once you have an area set up for this kind of dramatic play, minimal budget and staff time are needed to maintain it.

NOTE

1. Family Place Libraries, www.familyplacelibraries.org.

Chapter 8

Money Smart Week

FINANCIAL LITERACY STORYTIME

◇◇◇◇◇◇◇◇◇◇◇◇◇◇◇◇◇◇◇◇◇◇◇◇◇◇◇◇◇◇◇◇◇◇◇

ANGIAH DAVIS

Assistant Branch Manager | Youth Services Manager
Gladys S. Dennard Library at South Fulton, a part of the Fulton County
Library System, Union City, Georgia

LIBRARY TYPE	Public library

ABOUT THE LIBRARY

The Gladys S. Dennard Library at South Fulton, a 25,000-square-foot facility located in Union City, Georgia, is a branch within the large metropolitan Fulton County Library System. The branch is staffed by three full-time librarians, four full-time library associates, and three full-time library assistants. The working-class community is diverse in age with a number of daycares and elementary, middle, and high schools, as well as a college.

ABOUT THE PROGRAM

Each year, during Money Smart Week, the library collaborates with financial industry partners to host a Money Smart Kids Read event where kids and parents learn about money concepts during storytime in a fun and educational way.

TARGET AUDIENCE	Kids (ages 3–7)
PROGRAM BUDGET	Free

Our library system made Money Smart Week a priority, and our branch runs a Money Smart Kids Read financial literacy storytime each year as part of the annual initiative. The goal of this program is to expose young learners to money concepts in a fun but meaningful way. By working with the state coordinator for Money Smart Week Georgia, the library system was able to partner with the financial institution Country Financial, which provided the library system with several copies of the 2016 Money Smart Kids Read selection: *Start Saving, Henry!* by Nancy Carlson. Some branches had a Country Financial representative present at the Money Smart Kids Read events to read *Start Saving, Henry!* to children and their parents. The representatives also assisted with crafts and answered questions about money. Country Financial also provided flyers and posters to help us promote Money Smart Week programs.

While the selected title was read during storytime, children also participated in hands-on activities to reinforce Money Smart concepts. For example, some librarians provided children with ceramic piggy banks that the children could decorate with paint and take home to begin saving money. Other librarians held programs where children could play money games such as Monopoly and the game of store—pretending to purchase an item with real or fake money to help children understand how to count money and determine if they have enough money to purchase an item. Coloring sheets and money worksheets are also affordable options to help plan an activity for financial literacy storytime.

We suggest planning the program three to six months in advance. However, you can plan a program in less time. First, find out the exact dates for Money Smart Week. Each year, the dates change slightly. Second, figure out what you would like to do for a program and determine the goal or learning outcomes of the program. Would you like to have a one-time storytime? Multiple storytimes? Are you creating a Money Smart Week display? Are you having a discussion about money with parents and children? Date? Time? Location (where in the library or community center)? Intended audience? Third, select a date for your program. Fourth, order free literature from the CFPB, and search for materials on personal finance (budgeting, saving money, about money). These resources can be displayed on a resources table for parents and caregivers to take home after the program. This table can be displayed all month long, in advance of your program, during, and after.

Next, reach out to local financial institutions to see if someone can come out to talk to library users about money or even read a story about money to youth. The Money Smart Week coordinator for the state of Georgia coordinated the readers for my library. If you get a volunteer to read to youth, make sure the person is comfortable with reading to your targeted age group; not everyone is comfortable with reading aloud to forty-five pre-K students.

You may also opt to read to the kids yourself and have the financial volunteer just talk to kids about money or do a brief presentation about money. In our case, there were two financial representatives. One was able to read a story and serve as the cashier during our store activity. The other financial volunteer helped with the craft and took photos. It is helpful if your reader can read the book in advance. Consider having a copy of the book(s) for your volunteer to take home to review. Although you may be a children's librarian and you can read any story any time, some people cannot.

Next, create your flyers in January/February, and start promoting your event in March and April. Then create a Money Smart Week display for the first week in April. Your display can be for all ages or can be kid-friendly. I have used piggy banks, shredded money from the Federal Reserve Bank of Atlanta, Monopoly money, books about money, and financial literature for a display. Confirm your guest two weeks before your program, again the week before, and once again the day before.

Finally, some unexpected challenges may come up. Perhaps your speaker is unable to make the program or your staff person who is overseeing the program gets sick or has an emergency. Be prepared. You have advertised the program and do not want to cancel or reschedule. Make sure other staff members are aware of how the program should flow. Write it down if you need to, and have a backup plan in case your speaker or volunteer does not show. You do not have to have a special person come in to read to the kids; however, partnering with a financial representative makes the program more special.

Don't forget to relax and have fun! It's good to have another staff member there to take photos for you, or you can ask a parent to take photos for you if you are short on staff. You will also need someone to help you with crafts. Usually, I have the parents in the program assist me.

We were able to keep costs down by repurposing items already in the library. These items included books, posters, bookmarks, and cool library swag like mood pencils, pens, bags, and leftover summer reading prizes. You can always stock up on kid-friendly items at your nearest dollar store too, but set a budget before you go. By partnering with another organization, particularly a large financial institution, they are more than likely able to support the cost of items such as the shipping of books, flyers, and financial literature. Also, if you start in time, you may be able to get donations from an organization such as your friends group, a financial organization, a nonprofit, a store, or a community organization. The key is starting early.

We used a number of marketing tools to promote programming. These tools included Event Brite, flyers to hand out to patrons and display in the library, e-mail blasts, newsletters, the library website, social media, and the Money Smart Week website. All these marketing tools were free. The Money Smart Week website contains a free media kit for all Money Smart Week partners to use. Partners can download flyers, logos, and even social media post language. It's great to create a display to help promote the program and the Money Smart Week initiative.

You may want to create a handout or an electronic tip sheet for patrons with information about Money Smart Week, upcoming programs for the week, and hashtags for posting photos. Encourage patrons to post and like photos, and make sure you take photos of your program and post them as well. You can post on your library's web page or on your social media and/or submit to the official Money Smart Week page.

Through parent and teacher surveys, we learned that parents and teachers appreciated the financial literacy storytime and that the hands-on activity helped reinforce money concepts. My final words of advice are (1) know your audience; (2) make sure you have enough help, especially if you are doing a craft; and (3) participate each year, and share your story with others—both the challenges and the successes.

Chapter 9

Paint a Piggy Bank

◇◇◇◇◇◇◇◇◇◇◇◇◇◇◇◇◇◇◇◇◇◇◇◇◇◇◇◇◇◇◇◇◇◇◇◇◇◇◇

CLAIRE TIDWEL
Makerspace and Programming Librarian
Irvin L. Young Memorial Library, Whitewater, Wisconsin

LIBRARY TYPE	Public library

ABOUT THE LIBRARY

The Irvin L. Young Memorial Library is located in a college town that serves 7,045 patrons in Walworth, Waukesha, and Rock Counties of Wisconsin. We are a very involved town where there are many things for people to do. We host over two hundred programs a year for children, teens, millennials, and adults.

ABOUT THE PROGRAM

Children were given blank ceramic piggy banks and had to "pay" for their supplies to decorate them. Each child was given wooden nickels to spend, and they had to budget for the supplies they wanted. Did they want ten different colors on their piggy bank, or did they skip a color and get the rhinestones instead? Paired with a storytime of Rosemary Well's *Bunny Money*, young children ages three and up got a glimpse of real-world skills in budgeting.

| **TARGET AUDIENCE** | Kids (ages 3–7) |
| **PROGRAM BUDGET** | $1–$50 |

The program was held in tandem with the University of Wisconsin (UW)–Whitewater's Andersen Library's Money Smart Week, so we started the planning in December 2016 for the week-long event. Andersen's public relations and outreach coordinator, Sarell Martin, contacted Irvin L. Young Memorial Public Library for the partnership, and we were brought in to join a team of Andersen staff and UW–Whitewater faculty. We worked closely with Andersen library staff members, including Sarell Martin and Naomi Schemm, a reference and instructional librarian, to put on the program. They were providing programs and services for the students and faculty while we provided programming for families and the children's center located on campus. Our goal was to provide families with information about early financial literacy techniques by providing a fun program for the little ones while engaging an audience we do not normally see.

We divided the budget so that Andersen paid for the ceramic piggy banks and paints to be used at their location, and we purchased the supplies we would use at our location. We also ended up using our craft supplies such as sequins, rhinestones, and feathers that we had on hand already. We only had to buy the ceramic banks, which brought our program spending to fifty-seven dollars for three dozen banks from Oriental Trading.

Promotion was done by each party but was cross-promoted. Flyers were created by Irvin L. Young staff and distributed at both Andersen and the public library. Facebook events were created as well as promoted on other web calendars. Andersen targeted its faculty members who have children at the children's center, and Irvin L. Young targeted families throughout the community.

The event was modified for the Andersen location as we were using their children's space in the library during normal hours. This meant that we read two stories with a discussion about saving, and then children were allowed to paint the bank of their choosing rather than them "purchasing" their craft items to decorate with as they would have at our event. At the public library, we had the ability to expand the resources as we were located in a contained room and had fewer participants. Both events did have available age-appropriate books for checkout about money as well as literature provided by Money Smart Week.

We held the event on two separate days to give parents the choice to come to one library or the other. Irvin L. Young Memorial Library held the program on Monday, and it was then held again on Friday at Andersen Library on the university campus. Both events served the same purpose of informing children about budgeting and saving, but because of the space, we set up and executed the events slightly differently to make the best use of each location.

For the public library, setup involved organizing our community room for crafting. This meant that tablecloths were put down and tables and chairs were set up. The "shop"—which consisted of supplies presorted into Dixie cups for easy transport by children—was set up at the front of the room. Signs were placed so children knew how much they would be "spending." When participants first walked in, they selected their piggy bank and grabbed their wooden nickels, which were also presorted. At the university, tables were set for painting. Children were brought to Andersen from the children's center, and we first met for a story. They were then released to paint at tables that were set up by Andersen staff.

There are a few things to watch out for if you are planning your Paint a Piggy Bank program. As with all craft programs, be prepared for a mess. Having plates or similar items for children to take their banks home on was extremely helpful in containing the mess, as was having wet wipes on hand.

Presorting is going to be very helpful in keeping things moving fast and keeping kids happy. This is especially important with the paints so they cannot be overused or wasted.

Don't be afraid to be firm once an item is "sold." We had several children come up wanting to trade out items repeatedly. It is a great teachable moment in returns and item value, so use it. They were understanding, and they got to be creative with what they had. It also incites children to share. If a sibling was done with her piggy bank and had leftover coins, she was happy to share.

This program was a success and was a great partnership opportunity for both parties. The public library was able to reach families at the university that we do not normally see, and Andersen Library was able to put on a fun program for their faculty families.

Chapter 10

You Have Expensive Taste

◇◇◇◇◇◇◇◇◇◇◇◇◇◇◇◇◇◇◇◇◇◇◇◇◇◇◇◇◇◇◇◇◇

LESLIE SWOPE
Director
St. Marys Public Library, St. Marys, Pennsylvania

LIBRARY TYPE	Public library

ABOUT THE LIBRARY

Our library serves 13,070 residents in St. Marys, Pennsylvania. St. Marys is the second-largest city land-wise (99.52 sq. mi) in Pennsylvania but one of the least populated designated cities. The city's main industry is manufacturing, in which nearly half of workers are employed, giving the city a median household income of $48,419. The library has one full-time employee and sixteen part-time employees (six of whom are high school students). Our community is mostly middle-class people living in debt, and we are dedicated to helping them make smart financial decisions to allow them to retire well.

ABOUT THE PROGRAM

Have you ever heard someone say "I only drink Evian water"? Do you think name brands are status symbols that say something about a person? This program is designed to break down preconceived notions about what brands you like better by engaging users in a blind taste test.

TARGET AUDIENCE	Tweens (ages 8–12), young adults (ages 13–18), and adults
PROGRAM BUDGET	$1–$50

A brand is well known because companies spend a lot of money on advertising. The quality of a product is not necessarily tied to its fame or price. Many times, the most expensive brand is not the best-tasting, longest-lasting, or safest product to use. Generics or store brands are often a great way to save money on grocery bills. A recent study from the Private Label Manufacturers Association found that consumers save an average of 33 percent on the total grocery bill by buying store brands.[1]

We have found that teens, especially, are name-brand conscious. They want Nike because everyone else is wearing Nike; they must have Pringles chips and Mott's applesauce because that is what their classmates pack for lunch. By making teens try generic brands, they will realize that sometimes they prefer the taste of the generic. We hope that by starting with food, they will branch out and try personal care items and clothing that are not famous brands. We want to encourage saving money and using what you like, not what TV commercials say you should like.

This program cost less than fifty dollars. We did not partner with any other organizations, but a grocery store would be a great partner for this program if they would be willing to donate products or offer a discount. The money was spent entirely on food supplies. We already had small paper plates and cups on hand. We bought three versions of different food items: water, pop, cereal (Lucky Charms), peanut-butter cups, chips and dips, and ice cream. You only need a sample size of each item.

Setup included removing all packaging from materials. Products were placed on plates and in cups marked A, B, and C. Staff need to make sure they write down which products are A, B, and C. We created a chart on a sheet of paper with columns A, B, and C and rows marked with the product type (water, cereal, chips, etc.).

We calculated the yearly cost of purchase for each item if the buyer would purchase one package each week. For example, Reese's Cups are $3.95 a package × fifty-two weeks = $205.40; Aldi's brand is $2.50 a package × fifty-two weeks = $130. We also calculated how much money would be saved if the person chose the second-cheapest or the least inexpensive of the choices. Over a year, for peanut-butter cups, you would save $75.40 by switching to the store brand.

At the program, participants were instructed to taste each item in a product category. They were to think about what they liked or did not like about each item. They were to rank the items on their charts as one for their favorite, two for their second choice, and three for their least favorite. After all participants had their results, participants compared their opinions with each other. They were asked why they liked certain items better (flavor, texture, color, aftertaste, etc.). The product packaging was brought out, and participants guessed which was A, B, and C for each category. After the discussion, the actual products were revealed.

Participants talked about the price differences for the products. We discussed the cost of items over a year and how generic/store brands can save you money. We glossed over budgeting for grocery and personal care items. You can insist on buying a name brand for certain items (ketchup must be Heinz), but try to balance it with generic items (White Cloud toilet paper instead of Charmin). We encouraged participants to try new brands to see what they like.

Participants are usually surprised by the results. Filtered tap water has always ranked higher than all bottled waters, with Evian almost always the least favorite. This leads to a great conversation about the cost of convenience. Pricing out a cup of coffee at a coffee shop, versus a K-cup or traditional brew, is eye-opening for many.

The next time I do the program, we will talk more in depth about price comparing with bulk sizes. The larger-size bag does not always mean that it is the better price. Drinks should not be purchased as single bottles at a convenience store or from a vending machine; it is always cheaper to buy by the case. Stress to participants that they are paying for the convenience of it being cold and readily available.

We had participants mention couponing, which can be a great way to save money. However, we stress that a coupon might not make a name brand cheaper. Prices do vary from store to store, and many grocery stores put popular items on sale. A sale price partnered with a coupon could be a great way to get a deal on favorite products.

We advertise our events in-house with posters and flyers, on the library's website, and through Facebook. We had ten teens come for the one program. If you are doing a program for teens, stress the free food!

This program is repeated as part of a financial series we offer for adults. Over the years, we have had over fifty adults participate.

Some advice I can share is to make sure that similar products are served at the same temperature (all water has been either refrigerated or room temperature). Try to find products that are similar in looks. If your generic cereal looks different from the name brand, participants will know which is which. You can always blindfold participants so they cannot see the differences.

You can do this program multiple times trying different products. If you have a kitchen, you could try different frozen pizzas. If you have a regular group of participants coming in, you could try other products such as garbage bags or cleaning products. Try out different office products like pens and paper. Encourage people to try different personal products and share their findings with the group. This would be especially fun to do with a group of moms with small children. They could swap diaper brands. If your library subscribes to a review site or magazine like *Consumer Reports*, mention it to the group. Encourage them to make their own reviews, and see if the local paper will publish an article for you.

This program is a great way to get people to start thinking about budgets and easy ways to save money. It is fun, and people generally enjoy programs where you feed them and ask for their opinions.

NOTE

1. Laura Heller, "10 Secrets about Store Brands," *Forbes*, December 15, 2011, www.forbes .com/sites/lauraheller/2011/06/29/10-secrets-about-store-brands/#a5a192c7db00.

Chapter 11

Envisioning Your Future Self Poster Project

◇◇

MEG KING-SLOAN

Library Branch Manager

Chesterfield County Public Library, North Chesterfield, Virginia

LIBRARY TYPE	Public library

ABOUT THE LIBRARY

Chesterfield County Public Library has ten locations across the county. The library helps people transform information into usable knowledge. From small business and job search assistance to student support and preschool learning opportunities, we provide educational experiences through community engagement and a hands-on approach. The library supports learning through materials and access, but our future lies in creating and developing learning experiences.

ABOUT THE PROGRAM

Our library was part of a nationwide tour of *Thinking Money*, a traveling exhibition created by the ALA Public Programs Office and the FINRA Investor Education Foundation. As part of our programming, we hosted an Exhibit Kickoff and Coffeehouse event, where we invited teens and tweens to create posters using museum posters and photos taken at the event. The artwork the students created highlighted how they imagined their lives in the future. They then thought about the education and finances needed to fulfill their dreams.

TARGET AUDIENCE	Tweens (ages 8–12) and young adults (ages 13–18)
PROGRAM BUDGET	$251–$500

Our goal was to provide an early opportunity for teens and tweens to find out about the *Thinking Money* exhibit and learn about financial literacy. The planning for this program started about six months before the exhibit arrived at our library. The planning committee included managers and librarians at North Courthouse Road Library, including several who had contacts at the local high school and middle school. We discussed the idea of bringing in an artist to work with the teens and tweens on their posters envisioning their future selves. We considered using a high school art teacher but later decided to hire an artist from the Virginia Museum of Fine Arts to work with students on this project.

Our committee selected 6 p.m. to 8 p.m. as the time for this program. We thought this would work for both teens and adults and that a coffeehouse concept would be welcoming and casual. This event was open to all ages, so in addition to teens and tweens, we also wanted to welcome their parents and grandparents. There was no registration, so people could drop in at any time during the evening. The art creations were for teens and tweens, but all ages could make duct-tape wallets or sit at a table where they could write haikus about the theme of money and personal finance.

The *Thinking Money* exhibit was at our library in October and November, so we did most of our promotion after the school year started, particularly in the two weeks before the event. We worked with community partners including the local school system, the Virginia Museum of Fine Arts, local church youth groups, and the Home Educators Association of Virginia.

Our room was set up in three separate areas on the day of the program. One of these areas included several tables for prizes, food, and beverages. Another section contained groups of chairs for people to sit and chat, and the third was the area with tables and chairs for the art project, the haiku station, and the duct-tape-wallet area. We picked up the food three hours before the program and set it out thirty minutes in advance. Three staff members participated in setting up the event, and at the end of the program, there were two staff members who helped with cleanup. We spent our funds on artist fees, refreshments, posters, and other craft supplies.

Although the event activities were focused on teens and tweens, many parents and grandparents attended. However, the Envisioning Your Future Self poster-making project was limited to teens and tweens, and they all seemed to enjoy it. Many of the students became engaged in conversations during the project, even though they didn't know each other before this program. An artist from the Virginia Museum of Fine Arts brought in museum posters from previous exhibits, which the teens cut and pasted and reassembled with a photo of themselves that we took at the event. The resulting masterpieces they created showed that they had thought about the future and what possibilities it holds for them. (One of the teens had the caption "Future Vet" on her poster but then wished she had written "Future Zoo Vet.")

After this activity, some of the students were willing to leave their posters at the library so we could display them. We obtained permission from their parents, and we placed the posters on a bulletin board in the teen area. We received lots of positive feedback from people who came to the *Thinking Money* exhibit.

Another activity involved having a staff member demonstrate how to make the duct-tape wallets. We purchased duct tape in various colors, such as blue, green, and yellow. We found a pattern online and made a sample for people to follow. This was a popular activity.

At the haiku-writing station, people were encouraged to write about their thoughts on money and financial literacy. One of the adults wrote this haiku:

> Grew up poor. Without.
> Then, priority was SAVE.
> Now, breathing easy!

She left it with us, and we displayed it on an easel during the *Thinking Money* program. It inspired us as well as everyone else who saw it.

People were asked to fill out slips of paper with their name and e-mail or phone number, and these were used for prize drawings that were held every thirty minutes. Prizes included board games, coin banks, books, and other financial-themed items.

We used resources such as posters and bookmarks throughout the library system to promote the event. We also promoted the event on the library's website and Facebook page. The library assistants at North

Courthouse Road Library (the exhibit location) spoke to individuals at the circulation desk, inviting them to the program. We found these means of promotion to be successful because when we reviewed the evaluations, we saw that some people found out about the program because they'd received a personal invitation or found it on our Facebook page.

We didn't require people to register to attend this program, and for us, this was successful because people dropped in and stayed anywhere from ten minutes to two hours. Some of the local high school teachers offered their students extra credit for attending *Thinking Money* programs, so make sure that the schools know about your programs. When we displayed Envisioning Your Future Self posters that the students had created, it provided an opportunity to start conversations about the event.

Chapter 12

Harry Potter and the Prisoner of Student Debt

KATIE MOELLERING

Adult Services Librarian

Emmet O'Neal Library, Mountain Brook, Alabama

LIBRARY TYPE	Public library

ABOUT THE LIBRARY

Emmet O'Neal Library serves the city of Mountain Brook, a suburb of Birmingham, Alabama, as well as the surrounding area. We have one building with 40,500 square feet of usable space. The library collection has approximately 131,000 materials in various formats.

ABOUT THE PROGRAM

The Emmet O'Neal Library's Harry Potter and the Prisoner of Student Debt, a program series, sought to bridge the gap between financial literacy and young adult programming. The idea was borne out of our teen advisory board's desire for a Harry Potter–themed program that hearkened back to the library experiences of their younger days. When we received a Smart investing@your library grant from ALA and the FINRA Investor Education Foundation, we knew that we wanted to provide exciting and educational programming about finance. However, our teens thought that a financial program sounded dull, so our YA librarian, Matt Layne, went to the teen advisory board and asked for ideas. This series came out of librarians and teen members brainstorming until we came up with an idea we all liked.

| TARGET AUDIENCE | Young adults (ages 13–18) |
| PROGRAM BUDGET | $2,501–$5,000 |

Our program series was crafted for a grant we received, and we knew that we wanted to offer something for our teens much like the Harry Potter nights they had experienced as younger children. These were nights each year (usually when a Harry Potter book or movie came out) when the library was decorated like Hogwarts and librarians dressed as their true selves—wizards. We were able to use our children's department's decorations for most of the series and did not have to buy much more. It helps to have existing Harry Potter/wizard paraphernalia around!

The Harry Potter and the Prisoner of Student Debt series consisted of three main elements to meet the needs of our young adult patrons: (1) a fun craft activity, (2) a financial/educational element, and (3) a viewing of one of the Harry Potter films.

Each program in the series (including the film) lasted three and a half to four hours and required two or three staff members. However, this could easily be modified to fit a shorter time period by taking out the movie or craft and just doing one or the other. Also, some parts of the crafts could be premade so that so much time isn't being devoted to creating a wand or making a potion, but rather, attendees could decorate premade wands or mix premade potions.

In our first program, in January 2016, we introduced basic financial concepts to the participants. We had three staff members to assist in setup and the implementation of the program. Students received a budget that was determined by the wizarding family they aligned themselves with—students chose their houses and were assigned a wizard family. They could choose to be a Weasley and be relatively poor, or they could choose to be a Malfoy and be wealthy. They also received letters of acceptance from the Hogwarts School of Witchcraft and Wizardry, which detailed the yearly amount of tuition for which each student would be responsible. Students made wands for the craft activity and were sorted into one of the four wizarding houses. This program had fifteen young wizards in attendance.

In February, our wizarding students learned about budgeting. They were given Harry Potter–themed money and asked to plan their budgets.

They had to use the money to pay for all the incidentals that come with a wizarding education—do they need a racing broom or expensive potions books? Students had to figure this out before they moved on to our last activity—watching *Harry Potter and the Chamber of Secrets.* Sixteen teens attended this event.

In March, we brought in a college counselor to talk with the students about college costs and how to choose a college that fits their needs. She engaged the participants with a presentation and answered questions they had regarding choosing a school and paying for college. She gave the students several pointers on finding scholarships. We made butterbeer, and our young wizards watched another Harry Potter film. We also talked about the fact that because of changes in the wizarding world, the cost for Hogwarts had risen. We pointed students to our refreshed collection of books on scholarships, grants, and loans to help them figure out how to pay for Hogwarts based on tuition and their financial situation. This March program brought in twenty-six teens.

For our April program, the Hogwarts students were divided into their houses and worked together to temper chocolate in order to make chocolate frogs. Later, they were introduced to library databases that provide information for college preparation, career planning, and homework help. We also watched another Harry Potter film. Nine teens attended our April event.

At our May program, twelve students learned about interview and résumé-writing skills from two of our librarians, one of whom is responsible for hiring at the library. Wizarding students were asked to begin putting their résumés together. As they did that task, they were also pulled into "interviews" by library staff members for an imaginary position in the restricted section of the library. This gave our teens practice at résumé writing and an idea of what it would really be like to be interviewed for a job. Teens also had a smaller craft this month and watched a film.

June's program covered student loans, college debt, and credit cards. Our YA librarian pulled together information from ALA/FINRA partners to present to the teens. This was presented to teens while they put together a craft and watched another Harry Potter film. We heard stories from teens who thought that pyramid schemes were valid ways to make money or who already had credit card debt. It was a great way to find out what they knew about credit and debt but also what they *thought* they knew about credit and debt! Fifteen teens attended the June program.

In July, we presented our students with an opportunity to interview their future selves, a very Harry Potter activity! Just like Hermione was able to use the Time-Turner to save Sirius, we used the Time-Turner to bring in a panel of fifteen wizards (actually, former teen advisory board members) who spoke to our current students about their college and career experiences. Our participants *loved* this program because they were hearing from people who were five to ten years older who really had experienced all kinds of ups and downs in regard to money, finance, budgeting, interviewing, and résumé writing. Fifteen teens participated in the July program.

Our finale was held in late July (on Harry Potter's birthday, actually!) for students who made it through all their years at Hogwarts. We celebrated with a feast in the Great Hall (really, the library meeting room). Twenty teens joined us for this event. We ate lots of good food, sampled butterbeer and pumpkin juice, and had a birthday cake for Harry. Finally, we watched the last film in the Harry Potter series, and students went home with copies of the latest Harry Potter book.

One of the biggest challenges with any young adult program is to get participation. Teenagers in our city tend to have full academic and athletic schedules, so it is important to create an atmosphere that is fun and inviting. We attempted this by adding creative elements to the room where we meet and by creating flyers that are funny and eye-catching. We also made sure to advertise the programs over the school's morning announcements in the week prior to each program.

Advance planning was extremely necessary because this particular series was staff-intensive. We needed to find free, workable budgets online that would work for our purposes, especially for the first three programs in the series. Our YA librarian and teen advisory board members spent a lot of time pulling together craft materials and making sure that our crafts would be doable during the program. We also had to print materials like the Harry Potter–themed money and letters from Hogwarts. We used some teen advisory board members and volunteers to help with this task. For the most part, librarians led these programs and made the presentations, so it was a lot of work for our YA librarian.

The series was a huge hit because we were able to introduce financial concepts and put some of those concepts into practice while at the same time pretending we were wizards. I don't think that we would have had anywhere near the attendance we had at this series if we had just done a series on budgeting or colleges. Our teen advisory board members attend public or private schools where students already receive information about colleges and about 90 percent go on to higher education. So we really needed to find another fun way to get this information to them. For our library, Harry Potter and the Prisoner of Student Debt worked really well.

Chapter 13

Planning for Life after High School

◇◇

MEG KING-SLOAN
Library Branch Manager
Chesterfield County Public Library, North Chesterfield, Virginia

LIBRARY TYPE	Public library

ABOUT THE LIBRARY

Chesterfield County Public Library has ten locations across the county. The library helps people transform information into usable knowledge. From small business and job search assistance to student support and pre-school learning opportunities, we provide educational experiences through community engagement and a hands-on approach. The library supports learning through materials and access, but our future lies in creating and developing learning experiences.

ABOUT THE PROGRAM

This program for high school students and their parents featured a panel of speakers providing information on financial literacy topics, from college and internships to handling money wisely and preventing fraud. These speakers brought their unique perspectives to handling life's challenges, including financial ones, after completing high school.

TARGET AUDIENCE	Young adults (ages 13–18)
PROGRAM BUDGET	$51–$100

Our library received the *Thinking Money* traveling exhibit from the ALA Public Programs Office and the FINRA Investor Education Foundation and planned this program as part of our offerings during the display period. We began planning about six months before the exhibit arrived. Our planning committee included managers and librarians at North Courthouse Road Library (the exhibit location), including several who had contacts at the local high school and middle school.

We chose 6 p.m. to 8 p.m. as a good time for both teens and their parents to attend the program. This was the third of four programs associated with *Thinking Money,* and we thought that there would be people who would come to all our programs if they took place at the same time. When we talked to people who attended all the programs, it turned out that this did make it easier for them to remember.

The speakers for Planning for Life after High School were from different organizations, some of which were outside partners. These speakers included a university professor who talked about the college experience and internships and a representative from the Federal Reserve Bank of Richmond. Others were county and library employees as well as regular patrons of North Courthouse Road Library.

The library's meeting room was set up with rows of chairs for the teens and their parents. The speakers were provided a microphone and a projection system for their presentations. There were tables in the room set up with refreshments and door prizes related to financial literacy. One of the speakers was from the Federal Reserve Bank of Richmond, and she brought pens and other small items as giveaways. Because it was November, we provided coffee, hot chocolate, and bottled water along with wrapped snacks so there was minimal cleanup after the program was over. We had two staff members at this event, and they were able to manage setup and cleanup.

The program was well received by both the teens and their parents.

The five speakers went in this order:

- **College/internships:** A professor from a local university talked about the college experience and the value of internships as a means of getting experience and exploring a possible career choice.
- **Financial choices/how to be smart with money and avoid scams:** An outreach specialist from the Federal Reserve Bank of Richmond talked about financial strategies for teens who are on their own for the first time and how they need to make smart financial choices.
- **Career/starting a business:** A small-business owner/entrepreneur talked about how she started her own business after working for others and how she found a niche for her services and then developed a client base.
- **Military service as an opportunity to learn new skills:** This speaker talked about how students could get their college education or learn marketable skills while serving in the military.
- **Meeting life's challenges:** A Chesterfield County Mental Health Support Services staff member talked about the psychological changes that occur when a student moves away from home for college or career and how to cope with them.

The program was two hours, and each speaker was supposed to have fifteen minutes to present his or her topic and then allow time for people in the audience to ask questions. However, most of the speakers went over their allotted times, and when questions were added, the program ended fifteen minutes later than scheduled. No one left early, and all the speakers stayed so that after the program, audience members could go to them with individual questions.

For about a week after the program, I received phone calls from people who attended who had thought of more questions, and I contacted the speakers for insight and answers. The feedback I received after the program was positive, and the teens were particularly interested in hearing about the psychological aspects of leaving home for the first time. We spent our budget on snacks, drinks, and small prizes as giveaways for a drawing at the event. None of the speakers at this program charged a fee.

We created posters, flyers, and bookmarks to display and hand out to patrons throughout the library system, as well as using the library's website and Facebook page to market this event. We also contacted local schools, a homeschooling organization, and local church youth groups and left them posters and flyers. Library assistants gave personal invitations to patrons as they came to the circulation desk to check out materials. When we reviewed the evaluations, we saw that some people found out about this program because they saw a flyer at one of our branches or found it on our Facebook page.

We learned from program participants that they had received information that they hadn't heard anywhere else, even at their high schools. You can tailor the topics your speakers will present for this program to meet the needs of your community. The composition of this group worked well for us, but having five speakers was a lot; you might decide to have three or four speakers instead. We were able to get the word out to local schools, particularly to high school teachers who teach social sciences or economics. Some of them offered their students extra credit if they attended the *Thinking Money* programs. This could be a good incentive for some high school students.

Chapter 14

Financial Literacy
for New Americans

◇◇◇◇◇◇◇◇◇◇◇◇◇◇◇◇◇◇◇◇◇◇◇◇◇◇◇◇◇◇◇◇◇◇◇◇◇◇

ANDREA FISHER

Librarian
Lakewood Public Library, Lakewood, Ohio

LIBRARY TYPE	Public library

ABOUT THE LIBRARY

Lakewood Public Library is an inner-ring suburb and serves the city of Lakewood as well as neighboring communities in Greater Cleveland. The library's convenient hours and its easy access on a major bus route attract people from across the region. Lakewood is a diverse, densely populated city of over 50,000 people. Historically, Lakewood has been a haven for new Americans since Slovaks and Eastern Europeans came to the Birdtown neighborhood of Lakewood to work at the National Carbon Company in the 1890s. In the latter part of the twentieth century, this neighborhood saw an influx of immigrants from the Middle East, Albania, and other Eastern European countries. Today, many of Birdtown's inhabitants come from Burma and Nepal.

ABOUT THE PROGRAM

As a host site for the *Thinking Money* exhibit offered by the ALA Public Programs Office and the FINRA Investor Education Foundation, Lakewood Public Library partnered with Asian Services in Action (ASIA) Inc. to present two workshops for new Americans from Southeast Asia, one with a

Burmese-speaking interpreter and one with a Nepali-speaking interpreter. For many who attended, this was their first introduction to basic financial literacy skills such as banking, budgeting, and credit.

TARGET AUDIENCE	Young adults (ages 13–18) and adults
PROGRAM BUDGET	$251–$500

Lakewood Public Library was awarded *Thinking Money*, which also included a $1,000 stipend to support programming. *Thinking Money* aimed to "teach tweens, teens and their parents, caregivers and educators about financial literacy topics—like saving, spending and avoiding fraud," so we sought to reach out to some of the underserved populations within our community.

Making the library a welcoming place for new Americans is one of our goals in the library's strategic plan, so it made sense for the library to target Lakewood's new Americans as part of the *Thinking Money* exhibit and accompanying programming. In addition to making our new American neighbors feel welcome in the library, a program on financial literacy would also help them learn to make better decisions with managing their money.

Lakewood Public Library is fortunate enough to have many great community partnerships in Lakewood and Greater Cleveland. The Madison Branch of Lakewood Public Library is in the Birdtown area, an enclave to recent immigrants from Southeast Asia, and is a regular meeting place for ASIA Inc. ASIA Inc. is a nonprofit organization based in northeast Ohio that focuses on health and social services for Asian Americans and Pacific Islanders. They connect the Asian American community with a variety of services including health, legal, mentoring, food, and financial assistance. It was natural to reach out to ASIA Inc. to not only conduct these programs in native languages but also strengthen their organization's ties within the community they serve.

ASIA Inc. has worked with the library in the past to host meetings and health screenings at the Madison Branch of Lakewood Public Library; because this branch is in close proximity to many of their clients, we held the workshops at this branch. I reached out to ASIA Inc. more than a year before the actual programs to get their support as a partner during the application phase of the *Thinking Money* grant. The details were worked out with the assistant director of self-sufficiency at ASIA Inc. about three months before the program.

Originally, I had thought that the library would host one workshop on financial literacy for new Americans. However, in working with a partner organization with a better knowledge of this community's needs, they recommended two workshops in two languages to better serve our new American neighbors; one workshop would be for Burmese and Karen speakers and another for Nepali speakers. We spent our funds for the program on fees for two interpreters and their mileage to the library.

In addition to presenting the workshop, ASIA Inc. also handled obtaining photo releases from all the workshop participants. Although we had a regular photo release form that we typically use for library programs, it was important that the participants understood what they were signing, so ASIA Inc. provided photo release forms in the native languages of the target audiences.

The workshops were held in an intimate meeting room in the branch. The manager of the Madison Branch hosted the event; we greeted people, made copies of handouts, and grabbed extra chairs as the program began to fill up. In addition to the assistant director of self-sufficiency and the interpreter, ASIA Inc. brought in another volunteer to assist with handing out papers, completing paperwork, and so on.

Because the library had never done a program like this, we were unsure of what attendance would be like. We had to bring in extra chairs to accommodate all the participants. In both programs combined, there were more than forty attendees, with both men and women of all ages. As an observer, I saw participants were engaged, inquisitive, and eager to learn about managing money and establishing themselves financially in the United States. Attendees asked questions and participated in exercises that helped them understand financial literacy basics. Also, having these workshops presented by people within the Asian community allowed the attendees to be more comfortable, and they trusted the information and insight provided by the organization and interpreters. Although some of the participants were familiar with the Madison Branch, there were several who had never been in the library before the workshops. Staff members from ASIA Inc. were also very pleased with the attendance and participation in the workshops and expressed an interest in conducting future financial literacy workshops at the library. These programs were highlighted on the ASIA Inc. website and on their social media pages.

We promoted the financial literacy workshops for new Americans in our traditional library marketing outlets: on flyers inside the library, on social media, in the library's program guide, and in our community newspaper beginning about a month before the programs and launch of the *Thinking Money* exhibit. However, knowing that our target audience probably had low English proficiency, ASIA Inc. also reached out to their clients to promote the programs.

I learned that the library can successfully engage underserved and non-English-speaking populations with the help and expertise of an outside partner like ASIA Inc. Having the library provide the space and pay the interpreters meant that people who had never been exposed to financial literacy basics were able to receive relevant and vital information that would help ensure their financial success and livelihood in America. Also, they saw a welcoming facility and staff that could help them with other information needs in the future.

In the future, I would consider working with ASIA Inc. to provide more in-depth and detailed workshops because the topic of financial literacy is so broad and there are so many facets to discuss. My advice for my library peers who are interested in holding a similar program would be to reach out to community partners who have an already-established relationship with the population that you are trying to reach. Not only do these organizations have a rapport with the people they serve; they often need space and support to further their missions, which is something that most libraries can easily provide.

Chapter 15

Money Smart Week at a Community College

◇◇◇◇◇◇◇◇◇◇◇◇◇◇◇◇◇◇◇◇◇◇◇◇◇◇◇◇◇◇◇◇◇◇◇

PRISCILLA DICKERSON

Cataloging Librarian

Atlanta Technical College Library, Atlanta, Georgia

LIBRARY TYPE	Academic/community college library

ABOUT THE LIBRARY

The Atlanta Technical College Library serves more than four thousand nontraditional community college students each semester. The student population is 82 percent African American, and more than 90 percent of the student population receives Pell Grants. Many who receive Pell Grants also apply for student loans, which amounts to massive debt. Three full-time librarians, one part-time librarian, and one full-time library assistant staff our library.

ABOUT THE PROGRAM

Imagining a Debt-Free Future was designed for college students of all ages and provided participants and family members with ways to finance their education without incurring debt. Our campus financial aid director presented this session to our current and prospective students. It was one of several offerings during Money Smart Week.

TARGET AUDIENCE	Young adults (ages 13–18) and adults
PROGRAM BUDGET	$51–$100

We started by learning as much as possible about Money Smart Week to determine if the campaign would be beneficial to the Atlanta Technical College community. I attended an information session held at the Atlanta Federal Reserve Bank in February 2015. During this session, a wealth of information, resources, and personal testimonies was presented to participants. In addition, various business partners in attendance offered their assistance to library representatives in the form of free guidance, advice, materials, and presentation speakers who would present for free. This alone is a dream come true for most librarians who regularly organize and facilitate library programming with limited budgets. The entire meeting was centered on supporting each organization in executing a successful and effective program. Needless to say, I left this meeting invigorated, energized, and ready to find ways in which I could help my community better manage their finances.

Immediately after returning to my institution, I created and submitted to my library director a program proposal for presenting a series of financial literacy programming at our library. Many in our community experience generational poverty. My primary goal was to present these programs as informative resources that would aid in better financial planning and increased awareness among individuals and families. Although the college's student body was the targeted audience for the presentations, they were open to the public.

Upon program approval, staff held a planning session where we discussed goals, objectives, activities, resources, and the budget. Some of the information discussed was placed on a planning chart that would be used as our guide during the planning phase. The initial chart was very basic and somewhat vague; however, it was later developed into something that better represented the goals and objectives we wanted to achieve for our financial literacy programming.

During this phase, I made good use of the available online ALA Money Smart Week's media toolkits.[1] Library staff members and the library director were each given assigned tasks. In order to garner more support for this program, we reached out to faculty, staff, and administrators. We communicated with various campus departments while reaching out to local community partners and businesses in search of speakers and presenters. This proved to be a successful tactic as the library was able to schedule an array of presenters representing a financial advisement company, a nonprofit financial organization, AARP, the campus financial aid department, and our campus accounting department. After securing and scheduling presenters, I e-mailed letters to each confirming their commitment to present along with all other relevant information.

As it concerns the budget, it is important to note that the Money Smart Week campaign encourages institutions to secure presenters who will participate at no cost to the institution or organizers. This not only aids in keeping costs at a minimum but also reinforces the goal of being money-smart. In addition, we were able to order financial literacy materials from the CFPB. The materials were given to us free of charge as a participating Money Smart Week library.

Our local Money Smart Week Georgia campaign organizer and campaign chair further assisted with our efforts by providing one-on-one advice and guidance, additional materials, constant words of encouragement, and community connections. The library director contacted our campus communications director for support and approval of all Money Smart Week public relations activities such as flyers, e-mail communications, use of campus information monitors, campus social media blurbs, and a press release. The media kit we used included template samples for the aforementioned. In addition, the usage of the Money Smart Week Georgia calendar proved to be very effective as certain community attendees indicated that they learned about our programming through the online calendar. I also created several book displays and designed display boards promoting the week. The promotional items created were strategically placed through the Atlanta Technical College campus. Our budget for the entire Money Smart Week programming was approximately one hundred dollars, which covered printing, refreshments, door prizes, and a gift bag for each presenter.

For the Imagining a Debt-Free Future and Smart Money versus Dumb Money: Investing 101 programs, the presenter was asked to inform us of any presentation and session needs in advance. This information assisted us with preparing for their presentations. We used the library's digital classroom and tested all presentation equipment (LCD projector, audio devices, screen, and computer) to ensure that they were operable and in good working condition. I also created a sign-in sheet and printed several Money Smart Week surveys, which were later used as feedback that would help shape future sessions and program planning efforts.

Before I introduced the speaker, I provided the audience with a brief summary of Money Smart Week, our campus's financial literacy programs, and our program intent. Those who attended these programs were actively engaged while the presenter provided information about multiple resources.

Before and at the end of the program, audience members were encouraged to complete surveys in order to provide feedback to program organizers. The surveys originated from one of the Money Smart Week toolkits and included questions centered on each participant's age, education, gender, and ethnicity; the value of the session to the participant; and suggestions for future events. We also received verbal feedback from some participants.

All feedback was later discussed and reviewed by those involved with program planning and assessment. In these meetings, we were able to evaluate our program and target a number of issues. Overall, those who participated in the session conveyed through their surveys that the session was useful and relevant. As a partner for the Money Smart Week campaign, we were asked to submit all surveys to our local state organizer.

This session was the first Money Smart Week program presented at our college, and I learned some valuable programing lessons:

- Market programs to the general college community but also collaborate with specific instructors and program directors to secure a guaranteed audience. For example, in looking back, I now see that this program may appeal more to students who are in our dual-enrollment program.
- Better collaboration may have led to better attendance outcomes. In addition, collaborate with department heads to determine the best periods to host programming.

Overall, these sessions were enlightening in many ways. My advice to others includes the following:

- Start early.
- Customize financial literacy programming.

- Partner with a financial institution.
- Collaborate, collaborate, collaborate.
- Create a budget and stick with it.
- Market and promote programming aggressively, be specific, and focus on a target audience.
- Communicate beforehand with presenters on all presentation needs.
- Involve the entire community.
- Find ways to thank your presenters (e.g., gift bags, school paraphernalia).
- Keep it fun and educational.
- Offer door prizes, snacks, and other incentives.

NOTE

1. ALA Money Smart Week, www.ala.org/aboutala/offices/money-smart-week.

Chapter 16

Financial Literacy Fair

◇◇◇◇◇◇◇◇◇◇◇◇◇◇◇◇◇◇◇◇◇◇◇◇◇◇◇◇◇◇◇◇◇◇◇◇◇◇◇

CURT FRIEHS
Director of Library Services
Vaughn College, Flushing, New York, and
Former Business Librarian
SUNY Old Westbury Library, Old Westbury, New York

LIBRARY TYPE	Academic library

ABOUT THE LIBRARY

SUNY Old Westbury Library serves a community of approximately five thousand students. We also serve older, nontraditional students and college employees. As a state school, the general public can access our campus as well.

ABOUT THE PROGRAM

Launched in 2018, the Financial Literacy Fair is an annual event hosted in April to better inform students of their options and enable them to make more informed financial decisions. We typically schedule the fair in early April; later in the month, students are busy studying for finals.

TARGET AUDIENCE	Adults
PROGRAM BUDGET	$5,000+

Oftentimes college is the first time that younger adults are exposed to student loans, credit cards, and managing their personal finances. In many ways, it's a critical moment. Financial decisions made in one's late teens and early twenties can have a tremendous long-term impact. Getting started on the right track for financial success can literally make all the difference.

The goal of hosting our Financial Literacy Fair is to make financial literacy fun. Students learn about personal finance and are consequently in better financial shape as a result of our efforts. Good things take time. To that end, planning for the April fair starts over six months in advance, at the beginning of the fall semester. Ideally, librarians will find others to collaborate with on campus.

We invited many speakers and vendors. Twenty vendors such as banks, credit unions, and insurance companies came to campus to staff informational booths. These speakers touched on a number of personal finance topics such as college financial aid counseling, financial planning, health and life insurance, identity theft, retirement, real estate, student loans, tax issues, and other financial literacy–related topics. As a business librarian, I participated in presentations, served as a session moderator, and promoted library financial literacy resources.

In many ways, our guest presenters were the stars of the fair. Under no obligation to sell or promote financial services, they were honest and spoke candidly about personal finance and their backgrounds. Our most engaging presenters could relate to students and often had fascinating journeys that led them to work in the financial services industry. One presenter grew up poor in New York City. He talked about financial goals, planning, and dreams of a better life. Students can relate to these stories. We found that financial institutions are often willing to send guest speakers to such events. This creates a win-win situation for college students, presenters, and librarians.

Our facilities and janitorial staff set up tables, chairs, and a podium in our presentation room. We had over a dozen staff volunteers at various times. We assigned various staff volunteers to moderate sessions. Prior to the fair, presenters and staff volunteers exchanged contact information and established contact. Volunteer moderators prepared questions for their sessions and learned about guest presenter backgrounds so they could properly introduce speakers on fair day.

Most of our budget went toward food for fair participants—specifically, boxed lunches and snacks. They were a hit with students and went fast. We also had balloons, signage, and decorations in school colors. In the future, however, we wouldn't do box lunches again; it was hard to control how much food was being taken, and we ran out quickly. If possible, we would also choose another location that's even larger.

We promoted the Financial Literacy Fair in student newsletters, in mass e-mails, and on social media. We also put signage up throughout campus. The Financial Literacy Fair took place in early April. We started to promote the fair in early March. When students returned from spring break in late March, we increased our promotional efforts.

One measure of success is attendance. Four hundred and ninety students attended, as well as twenty-four faculty and staff. More important, students gained additional financial insights. The fair generated increased interest on campus. Perhaps most importantly, our financial literacy committee had launched a campus-wide event, and we wanted to continue to promote financial literacy in April.

In addition to the fair, we created a Financial Literacy at Old Westbury committee, which assists students who are having financial aid issues. To create the committee, I collaborated with business administrators and faculty, the college's associate vice president for business affairs and controller, the financial aid office, and other interested campus areas.

Some final thoughts on the Financial Literacy Fair: plan ahead! If you get a lot of money for food, spend it in ways so that the food won't disappear so fast. Whether it's popcorn or wraps, avoid putting food in boxes so attendees take only what they need. If it's too easy for college students to take lunch for both themselves and all their friends, inevitably they will. Library-related financial literacy giveaways could be part of these efforts. Students tend to respond favorably to free pizza and school swag.

Also, get as many different people involved as possible. Financial literacy programming does not need to be held in the library. Indeed, given the number of attendees, food, and other aspects of a Financial Literacy Fair, it may not be conducive to having the program within the library. That's okay too. Finding ways to engage students outside of the library is a critical component of librarian outreach and success. These days, a librarian simply needs Internet access and a laptop to bring library resources to nonlibrary users. By establishing contact in alternative spaces outside of the library, it's possible to get students excited about the library when they may not be all that familiar with the physical library space.

Chapter 17

Smart Cookie Credit

◇◇

EMILY MROSS

Business Librarian and Library Outreach Coordinator
Penn State Harrisburg Library, Middletown, Pennsylvania

LIBRARY TYPE	Academic library

ABOUT THE LIBRARY

Penn State Harrisburg Library serves 5,000 undergraduate and graduate students on a suburban campus in central Pennsylvania. Our student body is diverse and on the move: 14.5 percent of Harrisburg students are international, and many students transfer between Penn State campuses or to Harrisburg from community colleges. Regardless of background, one thing is the same for all Penn State students—they are not required to take any credits in financial literacy education, leaving extracurricular programs to help fill in the gap.

ABOUT THE PROGRAM

Smart Cookie Credit introduces college students to basic budgeting, building credit, and good uses of credit through real-life examples from a financial professional each semester.

TARGET AUDIENCE	Adults
PROGRAM BUDGET	$1–$50

College students have many opportunities to borrow but may not be prepared to ask the right questions of a potential creditor or grapple with the outcome of bad borrowing behaviors. To set the goals for this workshop, I consulted the borrowing and credit guideline in *Financial Literacy Education in Libraries: Guidelines and Best Practices for Service* from the RUSA and selected the following outcomes:[1]

1. Understand the concept of creditworthiness and how it can affect your interest rates.
2. Identify good sources of credit for average consumers.
3. Have a basic understanding of credit scores, how they are determined, and how they are used.
4. Understand the importance of checking one's credit score annually, and demonstrate how to get free, reliable credit reports.
5. Understand how credit can affect access to jobs and housing.
6. Understand how to use credit knowledgeably and wisely.

When I first worked with First National Bank, which helps us coordinate our programming, we had a lead time of three months to select a date and determine the objectives and content. For subsequent programs, we work about a month in advance to select a date, update content, and begin to advertise. Over the next few weeks, we refine the presentation to meet the needs of our students. We also include some interactive and relatable components like memes and a real-life sample budget from our presenter's first postcollege job. The session gives an overview from a general perspective of interest rates, types of loans and credit cards commonly available from any financial institution, and financial education resources specifically available through Penn State for our students.

On a busy college campus, it can be difficult to select a time that does not conflict with other programs, classes, or opportunities. I selected two dates and time frames to accommodate the widest range of students—one late-afternoon session to target commuter, nontraditional, and graduate students prior to evening classes and one midafternoon session during the college's *common hour*, when no classes are scheduled, to target the traditional-age, residential population. We ordered snacks from campus catering to help entice students and developed a marketing strategy to help spread the word.

Partnerships help make this program successful and lower the burden on the librarian to be a subject-matter expert. This partnership started with the Pennsylvania Library Association's PA Forward Initiative, which supports libraries in promoting key literacies, including financial literacy, to their communities. As part of this initiative, the association works with literacy partners including government agencies, nonprofit organizations, and other groups that can help libraries provide literacy programming. At the time of this program, First National Bank was a literacy partner seeking opportunities to assist with financial education. I coordinated with a personal banker from a local branch to select a theme, set the outcomes, and refine the content. Our bank representative was the primary presenter and subject-matter expert during our event. Due to First National Bank's status as a PA Forward partner, I could be confident that my presenter would be knowledgeable and would not "sell" during the presentation, which can be a concern when inviting outside professionals to speak at your library. Instead, our session focused on financial literacy concepts and generic financial products available from any financial institution. We also incorporated financial literacy tools available to our students from Penn State University.

I used a number of outreach platforms to market the event. For college students, I find that advertising too early can be a problem, so I used a combination of long-term advertisements as well as advertising blasts closer to the program date. I created promotional graphics using Canva, a free, web-based graphic design tool that can optimize graphics for different settings such as Facebook, Instagram, and print media. I added the event to the campus promotional calendar, which displays events on digital screens across campus and secured first-year seminar credit for the session, which allows freshmen to satisfy extracurricular requirements; additionally, first-year seminar–approved events appear in a database for student preregistration. On social media, I created a Facebook event that we regularly promoted on our library page in the weeks leading up to the session. The event page also allowed us to post the first-year seminar registration link to encourage sign-ups. I also shared the graphics in our Instagram feed and stories, which is the social media platform most commonly used by our students. Finally, I utilized the student e-mail discussion list to promote the event the day before and the day of each session.

We spent twenty-five dollars per event on cookies and beverages from campus catering. (You could eliminate snacks or purchase cheaper ones to cut costs.) Surprisingly, our students actually did not eat many snacks, which are typically the main attraction at events. Our presenter was free. Financial institutions typically do not charge for educational events, as such events are favorable when regulators review the bank.

We used a basic-room setup, with rows of chairs, a podium with a computer, and a projector and screen. Two people staffed the event: the business librarian and the personal banker. We provided handouts with more information about financial literacy resources at Penn State.

In total, twenty-eight people attended two sessions. The evening session attracted nine people, and the afternoon attracted nineteen. We asked students to grade their knowledge of personal credit from A to F before and after the session. Before the session, students gave themselves B to F grades, with the majority giving themselves a C or less. After the session, students gave themselves A to C grades, with the majority of students giving themselves a B or C.

We also asked students pre- and post-test questions:

1. Name a credit reporting agency.
2. True or false? Your credit score is determined from your borrowing history and helps lenders determine how risky it would be to lend you money.
3. Select the item that is *not* a part of your credit report:
    - credit history
    - name, address, and Social Security number
    - income
    - all open and closed accounts with lenders

Prior to the session, most students could not name one of the three credit reporting agencies. They also had difficulty identifying information that is not part of a credit report. After the session, the majority of students answered all questions correctly. Based on this data, we did achieve our goals of increasing their personal knowledge of credit.

We asked students to rank the program in terms of helpfulness. All students said that the program was helpful to some degree, with the majority indicating that the program was moderately to extremely helpful. We also asked what they hoped to learn but did not. Only two students said that there was something they did not learn; one person wanted to learn more about interest, and one person wanted to learn more about the best credit cards to use. We amended the program to talk more about interest, but because we do not sell products during the session, we do not mention specific cards. Our presenter discusses securing credit cards generally as a way to build credit, which kinds of interest rates are reasonable, and which kinds of interest rates one can expect based on his or her credit score.

We learned that sometimes there is a mismatch of student expectations. To protect students, we do not allow selling in these sessions. However, some students want very specific advice. In these instances, we can point them back to their banks or a financial counselor, but it is not information we provide in the sessions.

My final advice is to find a trustworthy bank or financial institution in your community and learn about the programming they can offer. It takes the pressure off the librarian to be a financial expert and provides professional credibility for patrons. Make sure that they understand there is no selling, and review their content ahead of time to ensure that it meets your goals and expectations for the session. Our banker is flexible and works with us to create the programming our students want.

NOTE

1. Reference and User Services Association, *Financial Literacy Education in Libraries: Guidelines and Best Practices for Service*, 2014, www.ala.org/rusa/sites/ala.org.rusa/files/content/FLEGuidelines_Final_September_2014.pdf.

Chapter 18

Small Business, Big Ideas

◇◇◇

J. SANDY HUTCHINS

Head of Adult Services
DeLand Regional Library, DeLand, Florida

LIBRARY TYPE	Public library

ABOUT THE LIBRARY

DeLand Regional Library, a branch of the Volusia County Public Library, has been serving the residents of Deland, Florida, for more than one hundred years. DeLand has a population of thirty thousand residents. A significant portion of the population is in flux, however, as we're home to both Stetson University and several retirement communities. Our twenty staff members strive to promote the library to our changing residents. DeLand Regional Library offers programs for all ages, from bilingual storytimes for toddlers to computer classes for senior citizens.

ABOUT THE PROGRAM

Community members are invited to attend a free series of programs on small businesses. From the initial idea to the final execution, we highlighted what it takes to write a business plan, get a loan, promote your business, and more. Participants learned from the mistakes and successes of local business owners.

TARGET AUDIENCE	Adults
PROGRAM BUDGET	Free

In recent years, reference staff members have noticed that a growing number of computer users at the library with small or home-based businesses needed assistance. From landscapers placing ads on Craigslist to childcare workers creating flyers, we have identified a population in our community that would economically benefit from increasing their computer literacy and general business know-how.

This led to the creation of the Small Business, Big Ideas series. We began with polling both patrons and staff to determine what information was most desired by business owners (and those considering business ownership) in our community. Upon compiling a list of ideas, we discovered that library staff was not experienced enough in the topics to cover all the presentations needed. We would have to find knowledgeable partners from our community to come in for several of the programs. We reached out to many local businesses and organizations to participate in this series. In the end, we found most community members we approached to be happy to participate. We began planning the program in the fall, with the series itself being scheduled throughout the spring, with the bulk scheduled during Money Smart Week in April and concluding in May during our How-To Festival.

Library staff members teach computer classes weekly at DeLand Regional Library. Existing classes were reworked and new classes were designed to target business owners. These classes included topics such as Microsoft Office, smartphone photography, social media, and online sales. Many of these topics were classes we were already teaching; they just needed to be adjusted slightly to fit this new audience. For example, we had previously taught a class on using Microsoft Publisher to create holiday letters. For this series, the class was changed to show how to use Publisher to create flyers to promote your business. Our class on online sales discussed the differences between using Craigslist, Amazon, eBay, and Facebook. We found it to be popular with not just local business owners but also members of the community looking to make extra money by cleaning out their garages.

Some topics in this series required us to bring in outside partners. For this we sent out an e-mail to many local organizations (such as the Chamber of Commerce and Downtown Business Association). We informed all potential partners that we weren't looking for sales pitches, just informative presentations that would benefit the community at no cost. We found that most of the people we reached out to were happy to participate.

The partners in the Small Business, Big Ideas series included the following:

- **The Small Business Development Center:** This organization, funded in part by the US Small Business Administration, provided free speakers for the series on a variety of topics including "How to Start a Small Business" and "Getting a Business Loan." The speakers were very knowledgeable and gave informative presentations.
- **SCORE:** SCORE is a nonprofit association dedicated to educating entrepreneurs and helping small businesses. SCORE presented at the library on topics including "Writing a Business Plan" and "Marketing for Small Businesses." SCORE's speakers were retired local business owners who were a wealth of information for our community.
- **Chamber of Commerce:** The local chamber of commerce was a wonderful resource to both promote the series and find community members willing to speak on a variety of topics. Local business owners were willing to speak for free about their successes and their mistakes when starting their businesses. An informal roundtable discussion of local business owners was popular with both current business owners and people who were considering starting their own business. This presentation proved to be the one on which we received the best feedback. Attendees most appreciated the information that was specific to our area.

Scheduling and promoting the Small Business, Big Ideas programs proved to be the most problematic aspect of planning the series. When possible, we tried to schedule the programs on evenings and weekends so people could come after work or on days off. In our quest to reach members of the community who weren't necessarily library users, we promoted the events in the series throughout the community. This included putting up flyers in downtown store windows, around community colleges, and even in area bars and restaurants. One aspect of the promotions that we found quite successful was sending promotional images out to our partners in .jpg format so they could share with their social media followers.

We began promoting the series a month before the first scheduled event. This promotion began with a large display of financial literacy and business books in the library. Each book contained a bookmark we created that listed all the scheduled programs in the Small Business, Big Ideas series. We also talked up the programs at our tech classes and other adult events leading up to the series.

For the programs themselves, the library staff taught tech classes that were held in our classroom and used our eLab laptops. Because we teach classes weekly, this required no extra staff members or preparation time in planning the programs. The presentations from members of the community occurred in our auditorium. Other than the staff time needed to market the program and set up the room, no extra staff members were required. We also had no budget for the series, so we used existing materials and equipment for the programs.

Overall, the Small Business, Big Ideas series was a success. Programs averaged twenty-two people in attendance. The most popular program in the series was the Small Business Development Center's "How to Start a Small Business" presentation, which attracted forty people. The tech classes were less popular, with the "Excel Budgeting" class drawing only seven attendees.

In the future, I would recommend having a budget (though a small one) for the series so that attendees of the tech classes could be given a USB stick (with the library's branding) to save their work on. We did give attendees of the Publisher class several copies of their flyers to distribute. They also had the opportunity to e-mail themselves the flyers for future use.

Feedback on the series was positive. Community partners all responded that they would be happy to partner with the library again. Patrons who attended the programs found the presentations to be informative. The programs we held were open to the public with no registration required. For future series, I would recommend having registration so it is possible to follow up with attendees. This would help determine whether the presentations have proved beneficial to their businesses.

Chapter 19

Starting Over

◇◇

J. SANDY HUTCHINS
Head of Adult Services
DeLand Regional Library, DeLand, Florida

LIBRARY TYPE	Public library

ABOUT THE LIBRARY

DeLand Regional Library, a branch of the Volusia County Public Library, has been serving the residents of Deland, Florida for more than one hundred years. DeLand has a population of 30,000 residents. A significant portion of the population is in flux, however, as we're home to both Stetson University and several retirement communities. Our twenty staff members strive to promote the library to our changing residents. DeLand Regional Library offers programs for all ages, from bilingual storytimes for toddlers to computer classes for senior citizens.

ABOUT THE PROGRAM

Bankruptcy? Divorce? Relocation? Career change? No matter what life throws at you, starting over can be hard. We offered a series of free programs at the library on everything from budgeting to building credit to buying a home to help people start over.

TARGET AUDIENCE	Adults
PROGRAM BUDGET	Free

In an area that is home to many retirees and prone to hurricanes and the occasional economic downturn, our library staff has heard many a story about people having to start over. We have library users dealing with relocating, divorce, bankruptcy, career changes, and other major life events. We were looking for ways to help beyond just giving assistance on our public access computers. This led to a brainstorming session among adult services staff. We discussed the different issues we have helped patrons research and proposed as many ideas as possible on the most popular issues. Our programming librarian then found partners from within our community who could give presentations on these topics.

We found several local businesses and organizations that were happy to help. They offered free, informative presentations (and no sales pitches) on a variety of topics. Programs in this series included the following:

- **Credit 101:** This presentation, given by a representative of a local credit union, covered what credit is, why you need it, and how to get it. We found this program was popular with both adults who were facing (or recovering from) a bankruptcy and younger adults who were just starting out.
- **Eating Healthy on a Budget:** Our state university's extension office has a Family Nutrition Center that often presents at the library in the fall on a variety of topics for our Healthy Living Month. For this series, we had a nutrition educator from the university discuss tips and tricks to make healthy choices that are affordable. The presenter even brought healthy snacks for attendees and had a taste test comparing name brand and generic items, which patrons particularly enjoyed.
- **A Home of Your Own:** Another partnership with our local extension office led to a home-buying workshop. This class taught everything from how to determine what you can afford to the process of buying to avoiding predatory lenders. It took a very complicated topic and made it simple enough for anyone to understand.

- **Back to School:** The local community college spoke on going back to school. The presentation included what testing is needed to apply, the costs, and the different classes available. Not surprisingly, the most popular section of the presentation was on what financial aid is available and how to get it. Several patrons surveyed after the program said the presentation made them feel much more comfortable about going back to school later in life.
- **Résumé Writing:** The Goodwill Job Center in our community was happy to give a class on résumé writing. Not only did they offer an informative presentation, but the speaker was happy to stay as long as necessary to offer attendees one-on-one feedback on their résumés.
- **Couponing:** A local blogger taught a couponing class for the Starting Over series. This is a popular speaker at many libraries in our area, and we book her regularly. Patrons learned how to find coupons and how to get the most savings out of them. It was popular with adults of all ages.

Library staff also taught a variety of technology classes for this series. Topics included a budgeting class using Excel, a Cutting the Cord class on alternatives to cable TV, and a presentation on Traveling on a Budget. Most of these classes were ones that staff had taught in the past; they were just rebranded when included in this series. The Cutting the Cord class was by far the most popular of the series, attracting more than one hundred people. We actually had to turn people away, so I do recommend either having registration for this program or offering it multiple times. The Traveling on a Budget class lasted much longer than expected, as many attendees had their own tips (and horror stories) about past travels. In the future, we are considering a discussion group on travel because this program proved so popular and patrons had so much to contribute on the topic.

Although targeted at adults who were "starting over," we also promoted the programs to our teen users and to local college and university students who could benefit from the topics covered. The series was marketed at local businesses, colleges, laundromats, and recreation centers—basically, any place in town with a bulletin board received a flyer for this series. We also e-mailed out flyers in .jpg format to our partners and other area organizations so they could share them with their social media followers.

One surprising thing we discovered about this series is how popular it was with families. We had originally expected the series to be attended by middle-aged adults. Although we did have many middle-aged adults attend, we also had parents bringing their teens to many of the programs. Feedback from attendees proved very positive. Many felt that this series helped fill a gap of life skills that teens and younger adults weren't learning in school.

A recommendation I would make to others planning this series of programs is to encourage staff to attend events, if possible. We found that the information given in the class helps staff assist patrons on the public access computers (particularly the résumé-writing class). We have had several patrons inform us that they were hired after applying for jobs online with our staff's assistance.

Overall, the series was a success. The only change I would make in the future would be to offer concurrent children's programs. We had several adults with children who attended. The children were not engaged by the presentations and would have been better entertained by an age-appropriate program offered elsewhere in the library.

We intend to continue this series in the future and are currently working on finding presenters for new topics to include such as Getting Out from Under Your Student Loans, Online Dating Safety, and Smart Investing. Our adult services staff keeps an ongoing list of topics we help our patrons with so we have a continuing collection of ideas for future programs.

Financial Literacy Education in Libraries

Guidelines and Best Practices for Service

D eveloped under an IMLS SPARKS! grant with the Business Reference and Services Section (BRASS) of the RUSA, ALA, and an advisory team of experts in financial literacy education from the National Endowment for Financial Education; the Fond du Lac Public Library (Wisconsin); the Financial Services Roundtable; the University of Wisconsin, Madison; FINRA Investor Education Foundation; Jump$tart; Brooklyn Public Library; iOme Challenge; CFPB; and the Salt Lake City Public Library (Utah).

Approved by the RUSA Board, September 29, 2014.

HISTORY/BACKGROUND OF THE GUIDELINES

The impetus for the development of these financial literacy education guidelines and best practices for libraries was the growing need and demand for high-quality references services and programming in the area of personal finance, investing, and other aspects of financial literacy. These guidelines and best practices relating to financial literacy education in libraries are the final product resulting from a SPARKS! grant awarded to RUSA by the

Institute of Museum and Library Services (IMLS) in 2013–14. The project was established with an ambitious timeline. The project got under way in late October 2013 with the appointment of a director and working team and the selection of the advisory group.

The working team conducted an environmental scan to identify and assess existing financial guidelines and standards. Draft guidelines were shared with the advisory group during quarterly meetings. Feedback and recommendations for the group were incorporated to improve the applicability and accuracy of content areas.

Two meetings were held with the advisory group to share the methodology and resulting products and to invite feedback from this group of experts. A draft of the guidelines and best practices was shared at the annual ALA conference in Las Vegas in June 2014 and posted for public comment in August 2014. Feedback from the session was reviewed and the draft documents revised. The RUSA Standards and Guidelines Committee reviewed and approved the final draft of the document in September 2014.

Introduction: Guidelines, Literacy, and Libraries

Management of personal finances requires information. Different kinds of information are needed to safely and successfully earn, borrow, save, invest, spend, and protect against risk. A multitude of sources provide financial information, and these sources can vary widely in their opinions, reliability, and objectivity. Principles of information literacy should be integrated at each level of the financial literacy guidelines. As with other literacies, libraries are uniquely qualified to address this information need.

Financial literacy programs and workshops should demonstrate how to accomplish the following:

1. Identify, access, and compare financial information from a variety of sources
2. Critically evaluate the credibility, timeliness, and point of view or bias of financial information and its sources
3. Apply financial information wisely and productively
4. Use financial information ethically

Each content area includes program outcomes that can be applied to a variety of programs, workshops, and classes. Also included are suggested program topics. The intent is for these guidelines to be dynamic documents, adaptable, and flexible. These recommendations are intended to grow and change through the implementation process.

How to Use the Guidelines and Best Practices

Included with each guideline are potential program outcomes that will be more specifically determined by the scope of content and target audience for a program or workshop as well as some suggested program ideas. For example, when planning a workshop for a teen audience that is focused on understanding paycheck deductions, you would use some of the content broadly described in the earning guideline. A possible outcome for participants would be the ability to describe factors affecting take-home pay. Best practices call for measured outcomes, which in this case might be a preworkshop survey that assesses participant knowledge of paycheck deductions for FICA, Social Security, and state and federal taxes. A postprogram survey would demonstrate a change in participant knowledge of those topics.

ACKNOWLEDGMENT

Financial Literacy Education in Libraries: Guidelines and Best Practices for Service was created by a working team drawn from the Business Reference and Services Section (BRASS) of RUSA, under the direction of an advisory group of experts in financial literacy.

Financial Literacy Education in Libraries: Guidelines and Best Practices for Service is also available online at www.ala.org/rusa/sites/ala.org.rusa/files/content/FLEGuidelines_Final_September_2014.pdf.

Working Team

- Kit Keller, project director, Independent Library Consultant
- Chris LeBeau, BRASS past chair, University of Missouri–Kansas City
- Elizabeth Malafi, BRASS member at large, Middle Country Public Library
- Andy Spackman, BRASS chair, Brigham Young University

Advisory Group

- Ted Beck, National Endowment for Financial Education
- Lori Burgess, Fond du Lac Public Library
- Judy Chapa, Financial Services Roundtable
- Kristin Eschenfelder, University of Wisconsin–Madison
- Robert Ganem, FINRA Investor Education Foundation
- Chris LeBeau, University of Missouri–Kansas City
- Laura Levine, Jump$tart Coalition for Personal Financial Literacy
- Elizabeth Malafi, Middle Country Public Library
- Kerwin Pilgrim, Brooklyn Public Library
- Adi Redzic, iOme Challenge
- Dan Rutherford, Consumer Financial Protection Bureau
- John Spears, Salt Lake City Public Library

Chapter 20

Earning Guideline

BROAD CONTENT AREAS

The guideline on earning seeks to inform audiences about earned and unearned income and total compensation.

Earned income is generated from wages, tips, salaries, and commissions. Unearned income is derived from other sources such as interest, rents, capital gains, and dividends.

People choose jobs or careers for which they are qualified based on the income they expect to earn and the benefits they expect to receive. People can increase earned income and job opportunities by acquiring more education, work experience, and job skills. Job benefits may include health insurance coverage, retirement plans, legal benefits, and tuition assistance, for example. Career choices, education choices, and skills have a direct impact on income. Local, state, and federal benefit programs can also help with income needs for people who meet certain requirements.

Possible Workshop Topics

- Getting your first job
- Understanding paycheck deductions
- What if my paycheck is not enough?
- How does education affect income?

Potential Program Outcomes

a. Identify sources of personal income
b. Understand the difference between jobs and careers
c. Understand factors such as careers, education, and skills that impact income
d. Identify reliable sources of financial information
e. Describe factors affecting take-home pay
f. Understand how income affects lifestyle choices and spending decisions
g. Understand government programs, deductions, and the relationship between taxes and income

FOCUSED CONTENT AREAS

Business income is another sort of income. Business income can include rent from investment properties or profits from a business. A business can lose money as well as earn money. New business start-ups are particularly risky. Personal income and business profits are taxable. Taxes are paid to federal, state, and local governments to pay for government goods and services. Social Security is a government program that taxes the income of current workers to provide retirement, disability, and survivor benefits for workers or their dependents. Changes in economic conditions or the labor market can affect a worker's income or may cause unemployment.

Possible Workshop Topics

- How the national economy affects me
- Where do my tax dollars go?
- Starting a small business: What do I need to know?
- Small business taxes and deductions
- What to do if I lose my job

Potential Program Outcomes

a. Understand the impact the state of the economy has on personal income
b. Know about federal, state, and local taxes
c. Understand the difference between interest and dividends
d. Understand the purpose and function of Social Security, job opportunities, and government programs
e. Understand unemployment benefits
f. Understand how to manage personal finances during periods of unemployment
g. Understand profit and loss in a business

Chapter 21

Borrowing and Credit Guideline

BROAD CONTENT AREAS

The guideline for borrowing and credit seeks to inform audiences about issues related to managing credit and debt. There are times when a person's income does not cover necessary or desired purchases. Borrowing money or using credit may be a way to pay for these expenses. Consumers must learn to choose from a variety of sources of credit.

Incurring debt by borrowing creates an obligation for repayment on the part of the borrower. Consumers must understand the consequences of the nonrepayment of debt.

When securing credit or taking on debt, it is important to maintain reasonable levels of personal debt relative to one's income and assets. There are a variety of places where consumers can obtain credit. These run the spectrum of quick credit and predatory establishments to traditional banks. Consumers must know how to assess the terms and rates under which one borrows from these enterprises.

Possible Workshop Topics

- Bankruptcy pros and cons
- Understanding, maintaining, and improving credit scores
- When is using credit the right decision?
- Payday and title loans: A cautionary tale

- How to get low-cost or free credit counseling
- Cleaning up your credit report
- Correcting errors in your credit report

Potential Program Outcomes

a. Understand the concepts of credit and debt
b. Identify why people may need to borrow money
c. Understand the difference between credit and debit cards and their appropriate uses
d. Understand the concept of creditworthiness and how it can affect your interest rates
e. Identify good sources of credit for average consumers
f. Understand the obligation of repayment and the consequences for failure to repay
g. Know how to shop for loan terms and rates
h. Calculate simple and compound interest and the cost of borrowing
i. Calculate the interest for different types of purchases
j. Understand appropriate levels of personal debt relative to income and assets
k. Understand basic loan terms, fees, interest rates, and APR
l. Understand how credit card companies apply interest
m. Understand how credit card cash advances are calculated and billed
n. Demonstrate an understanding of the spectrum of sources of credit from easy credit and predatory loan sources to traditional loan sources
o. Identify what should be reviewed in monthly credit statements
p. Identify three types of credit (installment, revolving, open)
q. Have a basic understanding of credit scores and how scores are determined and how they are used
r. Understand the importance of checking one's credit score annually and demonstrate how to get free, reliable credit reports
s. Understand how credit can affect access to jobs and housing
t. Understand how to use credit knowledgeably and wisely
u. Understand the implications of bankruptcy
v. Have knowledge of laws protecting consumers in their use of credit

FOCUSED CONTENT AREAS

Credit and debt options vary by purpose. Different financial institutions offer credit and savings options for knowledgeable borrowers who understand the legal implications of credit and debt. Factors that impact debt management include its relationship to saving, planning, and budgeting practices. It is important to know the warning signs of excessive debt and to understand options for managing it. In the area of financing education, it is critical to understand the types of student loans, grants, and repayment options.

Possible Workshop Topics

- When borrowing is the right choice
- How to pick a mortgage
- I found my car—now what?
- Paying for college: FAFSA, Pell grants, Stafford and PLUS loans, and private loans

Potential Program Outcomes

a. Understand the best uses of credit and debt
b. Understand the time/value relationship of money and how it affects debt repayment
c. Critically evaluate a credit card or loan agreement
d. Differentiate between market lending rates and above-market rates
e. Identify different types of loans (secured, unsecured, cosigned, closed-end, open-end)
f. Demonstrate knowledge of the common types of mortgages
g. Demonstrate knowledge of the common types of car loans
h. Critically evaluate the fees and charges bundled into a car loan
i. Demonstrate knowledge of college loans, repayment terms, and failure to pay consequences
j. Demonstrate an understanding of credit bureaus and factors impacting scores

Chapter 22

Saving and Investing Guideline

BROAD CONTENT AREAS

The saving and investing guideline seeks to inform audiences about basic and complex concepts of saving and investing. Income that is not spent is either saved or invested. People might save for special purchases like vacations, anticipated expenses like home renovations, or future events like retirement or a child's education. Savings can be kept in a variety of accounts with varying levels of risk, return, and liquidity. The value of savings is affected over time by interest rates and inflation.

Investing is the purchase of financial assets, such as stocks and bonds, as a means to increase future income. Saving and investing require informed planning. An emergency savings fund consists of a small amount of money, usually in a savings account, that you do not have easy access to, intended to cover irregular expenses or routine expenses during a loss of income.

Investors accept the risk of assets losing value in exchange for the opportunity of gaining value—the expected rate of return. Returns can take the form of interest, dividends, and capital gains. The degree of risk and return varies, and greater rates of return are associated with greater risk. Market forces determine the price of financial assets. Market forces also determine interest rates and inflation. Different people with different goals will vary in their tolerance of risk and in their saving and investing portfolios.

Possible Workshop Topics

- Planning for retirement
- How to select a bank
- Planning for the unexpected
- Making smart financial decisions
- Emergency savings fund: How to build one
- Plan today for tomorrow
- Making my money work for me
- Introduction to investing
- Meeting goals through financial planning
- Bank or credit union: Which should I use?
- Hiring a financial advisor: What do I need to know?
- Understand fees and expenses associated with investing

Potential Program Outcomes

a. Identify reasons for saving a portion of personal or household income
b. Make a savings plan for achieving financial goals
c. Explain the value of an emergency fund
d. Calculate the rate of return on basic investments
e. Understand the concept of opportunity cost
f. Understand the concept of liquidity
g. Explain the relationship between savings deposited with a financial institution and the loans that institution issues
h. Differentiate common types of savings accounts at banks and credit unions
i. Calculate the effect of earnings and compounding interest on savings
j. Understand personal and employer-sponsored automatic savings plans
k. Understand the concepts of principal, interest, and inflation
l. Understand the time value of money
m. Understand the relationship between risk and return
n. Understand how investments can provide future income through interest, dividends, and capital gains
o. Calculate how much would be needed for retirement, factoring in existing savings, pensions, Social Security, and future expenses

p. Develop a personal financial plan based on short- and long-term goals

q. Compare savings and investment alternatives and select those that best fit personal goals

FOCUSED CONTENT AREAS

Saving and investing are facilitated by financial intermediaries like banks, credit unions, stock exchanges, and brokerages. Some government agencies and regulators, like the Federal Deposit Insurance Corporation (FDIC) and National Credit Union Administration (NCUA), facilitate saving, partly by insuring deposits, while others like the Securities and Exchange Commission (SEC) facilitate investing. Others, like the Federal Reserve, can influence interest rates and inflation. Government policy and taxation can affect the attractiveness of saving and investing. Markets react to news and changing conditions and require transparency. Bias and poor reasoning lead to mistakes that systematic decision-making can prevent. Making diverse investments is one way to protect against risk. Estate planning involves managing an individual's assets base in the event of his or her incapacitation or death, including the bequest of assets to heirs and the settlement of estate taxes.

Possible Workshop Topics

- Stocks, bonds, and smart investing
- Creating a diversified portfolio
- The stock market and the economy
- Government's role in the market
- Understanding mutual funds
- Estate planning 101

Potential Program Outcomes

a. Understand the concept of debt-based investments, like bonds, and interpret bond ratings

b. Understand the concept of equity-based investments, like stocks, and interpret stock quotes, ratings, and analyses

c. Compare financial investments like stock and bonds to alternatives like real estate and gold

d. Understand common types of tax-favored retirement investment vehicles, such as a 401(k) or Roth IRA

e. Understand how market forces determine interest rates, inflation, and the price of financial assets

f. Explain how people in different life stages and economic conditions might vary in their saving and investing portfolios

g. Understand the distinction between real and nominal rates

h. Calculate the effect of inflation on savings and investments

i. Calculate the present and future values of basic savings and investments

j. Understand the concept of mutual funds and indices

k. Understand the role of intermediaries, regulators, and government agencies in facilitating saving and investing

l. Understand how government agencies can affect interest rates and inflation

m. Understand how government policy and taxation can affect the attractiveness of saving and investing

n. Explain how financial markets react to changing conditions and why transparency is necessary for them to function properly

o. Understand how diversification hedges against risk

Chapter 23

Spending Guideline

BROAD CONTENT AREAS

The spending guideline seeks to inform audiences about personal and household budgeting, purchase decisions, understanding consumer wants and needs, and avoiding the pitfalls of uncontrolled spending. Consumers cannot buy or make all goods and services needed. As a result, they choose to buy certain goods and services and not others. Consumers must prioritize, budget, comparison shop, analyze value, and weigh choices. Goods and services usually require spending money. Consumers can improve their economic well-being through informed spending decisions, which entail collecting information, planning, and budgeting.

Possible Workshop Topics

- Budgeting for success
- Building a budget: Wants versus needs
- Where did my money go?
- Comparison shopping
- Too good to be true: Becoming a savvy consumer
- Strategies for managing overspending and impulse shopping

Potential Program Outcomes

a. Describe the difference between wants and needs
b. Understand the purpose of a budget (spending plan)
c. Create a simple budget
d. Track spending habits
e. Make informed decisions by comparing the costs and benefits of goods and services
f. Demonstrate how to set financial goals
g. Demonstrate what it means to manage money effectively
h. Understand the ramifications of overspending
i. Know how to analyze and evaluate advertising claims
j. Understand what it means to live within one's means
k. Know that overdrawing a checking account will cost additional fees

FOCUSED CONTENT AREAS

Informed decision-making requires comparing the costs and benefits of spending alternatives. Spending choices are influenced by prices, advertising, and peer pressure.

People choose from a variety of payment methods in order to buy goods and services. Choosing a payment method involves weighing the costs and benefits of different payment options. Donations are expenditures made to charitable organizations and other not-for-profit groups. Governments establish laws and institutions to provide consumers with information about goods or services to protect consumers from fraud.

Possible Workshop Topics

- Charitable donations: Follow the money
- Consumer credit counseling: What can it do for me?
- Understanding advertising: How to avoid the seduction
- Buy, lease, or rent?

Potential Program Outcomes

a. Apply reliable information and decision-making to personal financial decisions
b. Understand the effects of spending decisions
c. Identify and understand the pros and cons of different payment options
d. Identify the benefits of financial responsibility and the costs of financial irresponsibility
e. Identify legitimate charitable organizations
f. Understand the importance of establishing and maintaining a relationship with a government-insured financial institution and know what it means to be unbanked
g. Know and use available consumer resources and make responsible choices by applying economic principles in consumer decisions

Chapter 24

Protecting against Risk Guideline

BROAD CONTENT AREAS

The protecting against risk guideline seeks to inform audiences about types of fraud and risk and how to manage personal information and finances to minimize their effects. There are many opportunities for consumers to open themselves up to identity theft and fraud. Consumers must recognize what makes them most vulnerable. People must be able to recognize potential fraud and ways to protect themselves.

Consumers need to build an awareness of ways in which finances are vulnerable to loss from unexpected events. Levels of risk are influenced by behavior and decision-making. Learning about different insurance contracts and products, including health, property/casualty, disability, and life insurance, will enable consumers to understand concepts of risk and insurance.

Possible Workshop Topics

- Understanding types of insurance: Which are best for me?
- How to protect your identity online
- Financial transactions on the Web
- When to shred and where

Potential Program Outcomes

a. Understand what type of information must be kept secure and private
b. Know how to protect personal information online
c. Identify how online activity increases vulnerability to identity theft, fraud, and other misuse of personal information
d. Understand the need to financially prepare for emergencies
e. Understand the basic function and purpose of insurance
f. Understand the key information—including risk, occupation, lifestyle, and age—insurance companies need to determine coverage and premiums

FOCUSED CONTENT AREAS

Advanced-level participants should be able to use the knowledge they have about identity theft, risks, and insurance to critically evaluate companies, contracts, and other resources and to describe actionable steps to prevent identity fraud, implement protections, and report suspicious activity.

Possible Workshop Topics

- Evaluating websites for safety
- Protect your computer using firewalls and antivirus and antispyware software
- Comparing insurance policies
- How to avoid insurance frauds and scams

Potential Program Outcomes

a. Assess situations that put consumers at risk for fraud and identity theft
b. Identify red flags that are indicators of identity theft
c. Evaluate advertisements and offers for legitimacy
d. Critically evaluate potential insurance companies
e. Develop and evaluate strategies that will mitigate financial risk

Chapter 25

Financial Literacy Education in Libraries

BEST PRACTICES FOR SERVICE

best practice is a technique or methodology that, through experience and research, has proven to reliably achieve desired outcomes. A commitment to using the best practices in any field is a commitment to using all the knowledge and technology at one's disposal to ensure success. The following recommended best practices for implementing financial literacy education programming in libraries draw on input from key informants, feedback from advisory group members, research conducted by working team members, and lessons learned from Smart investing@your library grant projects funded by the FINRA Investor Education Foundation.

ENSURE OBJECTIVITY: USE UNBIASED SOURCES

Libraries must take care to provide unbiased sources of financial information and maintain objectivity in programming. The personal and financial issues involved amplify libraries' obligation to provide patrons with reliable and impartial information. Libraries must be particularly careful to ensure objectivity when partnering with other organizations or individuals to provide programming. Implicit or implied endorsement of financial products or services, by libraries or their partners, should be guarded against.

This does not mean that all sources and partners must necessarily be objective. Values- or mission-based resources and partners can be highly relevant, authoritative, and effective. In taking advantage of these options, libraries can preserve objectivity by ensuring that diverse viewpoints are represented and that programming partners honor the parameters established by the library. For example, books advocating a variety of investment strategies can provide balance through diversity, and it may be that a local Certified Financial Planner would be an excellent presenter for a library workshop, as he or she clearly understands this is an opportunity for community service rather than a chance for new client acquisition.

In any of these situations, the library's responsibilities are best served by helping patrons to discern potential bias for themselves and account for it in their own decision-making. This by itself is a key element of financial literacy.

ENSURE ACCURACY: USE AUTHORITATIVE SOURCES

It is particularly important for financial workshops that inform the public to be accurate. Misinformation about interpreting loan terms or evaluating types of investments could have long-term consequences. Inaccurate information reflects poorly on the sponsoring library and on its potential partners. Publishers and authors of sources used in financial literacy education should be clearly marked, also noting relevant authority and credentials.[1] This document will recommend authoritative organizations and agencies.

ENSURE PRIVACY: GUARANTEE ANONYMITY

Communications with patrons regarding financial information must remain private. The personal nature of this topic increases the need for discretion when assisting a patron in person, on the phone, electronically, or at a program. Library staff must understand the sensitive nature of the topic and respect the patron's privacy while trying to provide the most relevant information. It is important to maintain confidentiality throughout the transaction as well as after the transaction or program.

ESTABLISH PARTNERSHIPS: SET CRITERIA AND EXPECTATIONS

A significant lesson learned from grantees of the Smart investing@your library grant program is the importance of establishing appropriate, productive, sustainable community partnerships. Every grant project has involved either establishing or expanding community partnerships, and these collaborations are critical to achieving successful outcomes and sustaining the financial literacy activities in the community.

As reported in *Libraries Connect Communities: Public Library Funding & Technology Access Study 2011–2012*, 50 percent of libraries report having insufficient staff to meet patron job-seeking needs, 57 percent report flat or decreased operating budgets in fiscal year 2011, and for the third year in a row, 40 percent of state libraries report decreased state funding for public libraries.[2] Partnerships are critically important to both the successful implementation and the sustainability of library-based financial literacy programming. Partnerships may also help establish or expand a library's position in its local community as a source of reliable, unbiased financial information.

Successful Partnerships Have the Following Characteristics

Mutually Beneficial

The most successful, long-lasting partnerships provide benefits to both parties. This may be due to sharing a mission or purpose or having shared or overlapping target audiences or because each partner fills a need for the other in terms of space, marketing skills, staffing, or other tangible resources. Partnerships are successful when both sides benefit and share a desire to support each other.

Partnership Established with Organizations, Not Individuals

While the initial contact with a partner organization is likely with a single individual, it is important to seek the support of the organization as a whole. This may be through a statement of support from the board of directors or the establishment of a communication network with the broader agency.

Many a partnership fails if the main connection is with a single individual. If that person leaves the partner agency, it often means the dissolution of the partnership activities.

Formalized Agreement through a Detailed Contract or Memorandum of Understanding

The contract document should describe mutual expectations in detail, describe the roles of both parties, include a timeline, identify benchmarks, and address the sustainability of activities.

Ongoing Communication

Effective communication is an important element for developing and maintaining successful partnerships. A process for ongoing communication should be established in order to nurture the relationship. This should include regular face-to-face meetings in addition to phone calls and e-mail communications. While the partnership is established with the agency or organization, it is helpful to identify a contact person at each partnership agency. An added benefit of these partnerships is the evolution of further opportunities for projects and collaborations.

Shared Target Audiences

A shared vision and a shared target audience are important aspects that support the sustainability of the partnership. These collaborations often allow libraries to address a captive audience, which can be both effective and efficient. For example, an effective strategy for reaching the hard-to-reach teen audience is to partner with school districts, individual schools, and teachers to incorporate personal finance content related to this age group into classroom activities or as library programs that earn students extra credit or count toward community service requirements.

Shared Contributions to Programs and Activities

Partners collaborate in a variety of ways, with both financial and in-kind support. A mutually beneficial partnership may result in an increase in community support in the form of donations of services and materials as well as funding. The increased awareness of the library and its services coupled with outreach to civic, social service, and government agencies leverage community support offered through a variety of mechanisms. Partners may take responsibility for carrying out important programming activities—such as marketing, recruiting, and providing presenters—and other tasks that help ensure successful implementation. This in-kind support fills the gap experienced by libraries in terms of adequate staff time and other limited resources.

BUILD ON SUCCESS: INCORPORATE CONTENT INTO EXISTING PROGRAMMING

Libraries have a long history of providing programming, training, workshops, and other outreach activities to meet the needs of their communities. ALA research demonstrates that "when the economy is down, library use is up. Unfortunately, at the same time, tight city and state budgets are closing library doors and reducing access when it's needed most."[3] This is not news to librarians, who are accustomed to "doing more with less." Smart investing@your library project principals have successfully incorporated financial literacy and education content into existing programming and routine staff training sessions. This, as it turns out, results in two important outcomes. First, this conserves time and resources, many of which are in short supply in public libraries. Second, this enables the successful implementation of projects and helps sustain the inclusion of financial literacy in ongoing library programming. This also helps to guarantee an audience, builds on existing marketing activities, and adds to the credibility of the content by sharing in the established reputation of the partnership organization.

For example, incorporating financial literacy content into popular storytimes or summer reading programs can be an effective way to address personal finance content for a library's youth audience. This minimizes the need for additional marketing and other publicity because the established programs generally have a captive audience.

MEASURE OUTCOMES: ESTABLISH BASELINE KNOWLEDGE

Once a program has been implemented and completed, it is important to assess the impact it has on an audience. A good question to ask is "What difference did it make?" Impact depends on several factors, including program goals, characteristics of the target audience, and the intended outcomes of the project. Measuring program outcomes provides information about the impact of a program or workshop.

Outcomes can be measured as benefits to people: "Specifically, achievements or changes in skill, knowledge, attitude, behavior, condition, or life status for program participants."[4] In order to demonstrate change, it is important to establish baseline levels related to content prior to intervention with project activities. Outcomes are directly related to goals, and both should inform the specific baseline data.

KEEP IT CURRENT: PLAN SYSTEMATIC CONTENT REVIEW

Maintaining an up-to-date collection is a standard library practice. In the area of financial literacy, current information is critical. As libraries prepare and present financial literacy programs and workshops, an essential step in the process should be the verification of the currency of the content. This might be accomplished through a partnership with subject-matter expert(s) in the field who have been vetted for bias and authority or through a subject specialist librarian.

PREVENT SOLICITATION

The library should establish and communicate a policy indicating that invited speakers should view a speaking engagement as an opportunity for community service, not an opportunity for business development.

PROVIDE SELF-PACED LEARNING OPTIONS

Sometimes what is needed is a place to refer people to self-paced courses that are provided by authoritative sources. To accommodate people's busy lives and different learning styles, self-paced courses are a good alternative. Among the recommended resources, there are options for self-paced learning in various areas of finance.

MAINTAIN BOUNDARIES

Librarians should clearly communicate their role as information providers and learning facilitators as opposed to financial advisors or counselors. When providing financial literacy services or programming, librarians should avoid giving specific recommendations regarding a patron's personal finances and financial decisions.

Librarians should also avoid making judgments about a patron's financial status, history, or future plans. It may be wise for libraries to maintain a list of professional and community services where patrons may obtain such advisement, although endorsement or perceived endorsement by the library should be avoided.

EXPLORE PEER-TO-PEER MENTORING

Students may serve as effective peer educators once they have successfully completed financial education training and assessment administered by a staff member and/or faculty advisors. They can help students understand budgeting, student loans, and credit. Libraries that host peer-to-peer mentoring should ensure that it complies with library best practices, such as confidentiality and objectivity.

NOTES

1. Lida L. Larsen, "Information Literacy Issues: Accuracy," Office of Information Technology, University of Maryland, revised April 2006, www.oit.umd.edu/units/web/literacy/Accuracy.html (site no longer active).
2. ALA, "Libraries Connect Communities: Public Library Funding & Technology Access Study 2011–2012," 2012, www.ala.org/research/plftas/2011_2012#final%20report.
3. ALA, "Libraries and the Economy," n.d., www.ala.org/advocacy/advleg/advocacy university/toolkit/talkingpoints/economy.
4. Institute of Museum and Library Services, "Outcome Based Evaluation: Basics," n.d., www.imls.gov/grants/outcome-based-evaluation/basics.

APPENDIX

Financial Education Core Competencies

The following core competencies were created by a working group developed by the US Treasury as part of the National Strategy for Financial Literacy and are used with permission of the CFPB.

FINANCIAL EDUCATION CORE COMPETENCIES

CORE CONCEPT	KNOWLEDGE	ACTION/BEHAVIOR
Earning/Income		
	Gross versus net pay	• Understand your paycheck, including deductions
	Benefits and taxes	• Learn about taxes and any workplace benefits
	Education enhances your earning power	• Invest in your education
	Sources of income	• Make informed decisions about work, investments, and asset accumulation
Spending		
	Know how to prioritize spending choices given available resources	• Set financial goals, track spending habits, develop a spending plan (budget), live within your means, comparison shop
	Long-term versus short-term implications of spending	• Understand the effects of spending decisions on yourself and others
	Appropriate purpose and use of transaction (checking) accounts	• Establish and effectively maintain a relationship with a government-insured financial institution
Saving and Investing		
	Understand how compounding helps saved money to grow Understand the time value of money	• Start saving early • Pay yourself first • Compare different saving and investing options

CORE CONCEPT	KNOWLEDGE	ACTION/BEHAVIOR
Saving and Investing		
	Know about federally insured savings accounts/certificates of deposit	• Build an emergency savings account
	Know about non-deposit investment products (bonds, stocks, mutual funds)	• Balance risk, return, and liquidity when making saving and investment choices
	How to meet financial goals and build assets	• Save for retirement, education, and other needs • Save/invest for short-term and long-term goals • Track savings/investments and monitor what you own
Borrowing		
	If you borrow now, you pay back more later	• Plan, understand, and shop around for a loan with the lowest rate and best terms for you • Understand when and how to use credit effectively
	The cost of borrowing is based on how risky the lender thinks you are (credit score)	• Understand how information in your credit report and your credit score impact you • Plan and meet your payment obligations • Track borrowing habits • Analyze renting/leasing versus owning assets (e.g., home or car)
Protecting		
	How to manage risks from potential losses or unexpected events	• Choose appropriate insurance • Build up an emergency fund • Consult a qualified/appropriate professional for help when needed
	If it sounds too good to be true, it probably is	• Avoid practices that are not in your financial best interest • Critically analyze advertisements and offers before acting • Evaluate advertisements or offers before acting
	Fraud/scams/identity theft	• Protect your identity • Avoid fraud and scams • Review your credit report every 12 months

GLOSSARY

Amortization. The distribution of payment in regular installments.

Annual percentage rate (APR). The annual rate charged for borrowing (or earned by investing), expressed as a single percentage that represents the actual yearly cost of funds over the term of a loan. This includes any fees or additional costs associated with the transaction.

Asset(s). A resource with economic value that an individual, corporation, or country owns or controls with the expectation that it will provide future benefit.

Bank. A financial institution licensed as a receiver of deposits. There are two types of banks: commercial/retail banks and investment banks. Individual consumers primarily use commercial banks, which are concerned with withdrawals and deposit services. Investment banks provide different services such as sales and trading, capital raising, and consulting to institutional clients.

Bankruptcy. A legal state where an individual, corporation, or government is released from the obligation to repay some or all debt, often in exchange for the forced loss of certain assets.

Bond. A debt investment in which an investor loans money to an entity, corporation, or government for a defined period of time at a fixed interest rate. Bonds are used by many companies and governments to finance projects and activities.

Budget. An estimation of income or revenue and plan for expenses for a specific future period of time.

Capital gain/loss. An increase or a loss in value of a capital asset such as investments and real estate.

Checking account. A deposit account held by an individual or an entity at a financial institution.

Collateral. Property or other assets that a borrower offers a lender to secure a loan.

Compounding. Calculating interest based on both the principal and the previously earned interest.

Contract. A legally binding agreement between two or more parties.

Credit. The ability of a customer to obtain goods or services before payment based on the trust that payment will be made in the future, often with the addition of interest.

Credit card. A card issued by a financial institution allowing the cardholder to borrow funds with the obligation to repay them within a specific time.

Credit limit. The total amount of money a credit card company will lend to a borrower.

Credit report. A detailed report of an individual's credit history prepared by a credit bureau and used by a lender to determine a loan applicant's creditworthiness.

Credit score. The numeric representation of an individual's creditworthiness based on income and credit history.

Credit union. A member-owned financial institution. As soon as you put money into a credit union account, you become a partial owner and can participate in its profitability.

Debit card. An electronic card that allows an individual to access funds from his or her checking or savings accounts.

Debt. Something of value, such as money, that is owed or due.

Deductible. The amount you have to pay out of pocket for expenses before an insurance company will cover the remaining costs.

Depreciation. When the value of an asset decreases.

Diversification. An investment technique that reduces risk by mixing a wide variety of investments within a portfolio.

Dividend. A cash distribution by a company to its shareholders.

Electronic funds transfer (EFT). Funds being transferred through electronic accounts such as wire transfers.

Endorse. To authorize the deposit or cashing of a check.

Equity. A stock or any other security representing an ownership interest in a company.

Finance charge. A fee charged for the use of credit or extension of existing credit.

Foreclosure. The failure of a homeowner to make payments on his or her mortgage, resulting in the repossession of his or her home.

Fraud. A criminal deception intended to result in financial gain.

Identify theft. When someone purposefully steals the personal identity of another, such as his or her Social Security number, financial information, or passport.

Index. A set of portfolios of securities representing a particular market or portion of it.

Individual retirement account (IRA). An investing tool used by individuals to earn retirement savings.

Inflation. An overall increase in market prices, resulting in the devaluation of a country's currency and of saved funds.

Insurance. A contract for a person or an entity receiving financial protection from an insurance policymaker. Examples include health insurance, auto insurance, and home insurance. Insurance is purchased by the payment of a premium.

Interest. The cost of borrowing money expressed as an annual percentage rate.

Investment. An asset or item that is purchased in anticipation that it will gain value over time.

Late fee. A financial penalty for not paying a bill on time.

Liquidity. The degree to which an asset can be quickly and easily bought or sold.

Maturity date. The date on which a debt or contract comes due.

Medicaid. A government assistance program for low-income individuals or families that helps pay the cost of medical or custodial expenses.

Mortgage. A loan for the purchase of real estate, usually secured by the property being acquired.

Mutual fund. A pool of funds collected from many different investors with the goal of investing in securities (stocks, bonds, and similar assets). Mutual funds are operated by money managers who invest the fund's capital to create gains for the fund's investors.

Net worth. The amount that assets exceed liabilities. Increasing net worth indicates good financial health for a firm and is key in determining how much an entity is worth. Net worth can be applied to both businesses and people.

New York Stock Exchange (NYSE). The largest equities exchange in the world based on total market capitalization and listed securities. Domestic and foreign firms can list their shares on the NYSE provided they follow the Securities and Exchange Commission (SEC) requirements (listing standards).

Nominal interest rate. The interest rate before inflation is taken into account.

Opportunity cost. The value of the forgone money, time, or other benefits a person could have received by taking an alternative action.

Option. A type of derivative security that represents the right to purchase or sell an asset at a preset price within a specific time frame.

Payday loan. A type of short-term borrowing where an individual takes a small loan amount at a high interest rate with his or her paycheck held as collateral.

Payroll deductions. A contribution plan where an employer deducts a specific amount of money from an employee's pay and puts the money toward insurance, health care, or an investment account on behalf of the employee. Employees typically enter payroll deduction agreements on a voluntary basis.

Phishing. A method of identity theft that occurs through the Internet. Phishing occurs when a false website that appears to represent a legitimate organization requires visitors to submit personal information to the site (via purchase or updating personal information). This information is then used by criminals for their own purposes or sold to other organizations.

Portfolio. A grouping of financial assets (stocks, bonds, and cash equivalents). Portfolios are held by investors and/or managed by financial professionals.

Predatory lending. Questionable actions carried out by a lender to entice a borrower into taking a mortgage with high fees and a high interest rate or that strips the borrower of equity or places the borrower in a lower credit-rated loan to the benefit of the lender.

Principal. The amount borrowed or the amount still owed on a loan, not including interest.

Privacy. A term relating to the use of personally identifiable information. Privacy prohibits the selling of consumer information to companies for marketing or soliciting purposes without customer consent.

Profit. The financial benefit realized when revenue gained from business activity exceeds the expenses, costs, and taxes needed to sustain the activity.

Rate of return. The amount of money generated by an investment before expenses like taxes, investment fees, and inflation are factored in. Also known as nominal rate of return.

Real estate. Land plus anything permanently fixed to it, including buildings, sheds, and other items on the property. Real estate is typically divided into three categories: (1) residential, (2) commercial, and (3) industrial.

Real estate investment trust (REIT). A type of security that sells like a stock on the major exchanges and invests in real estate directly through properties or mortgages.

Real rate of return. The annual percentage return realized on an investment. This is adjusted for changes in price because of inflation, fees, or other external effects.

Risk. The chance an investment's actual return will be different than expected. Risk includes the possibility of losing a portion or all the investment.

Savings account. A deposit account held at a bank or other financial institution that provides security and a modest interest rate.

Savings bond. A bond offered at a fixed rate of interest over a fixed period of time. These are not typically subject to state or local income taxes.

Security. A financial instrument such as a stock, bond, option, or fund that can be bought, sold, or traded.

Social Security. A United States federal program of social insurance and benefits. The program benefits include retirement income, disability income, Medicare and Medicaid, and death and survivorship benefits.

Stock. A type of security that signifies ownership in a corporation and represents a claim on the corporation's assets and earnings.

Taxes. A compulsory contribution to government revenue that is levied based on an organization or individual's income or purchases. Tax income is often used to fund government programs such as education, military, and so forth.

Time value of money. The concept that the present value of money is greater than the value of the same amount of money in the future. Based on the principle that money can earn interest and is subject to inflation, any amount of money has greater value the sooner it is received.

Transparency. The extent to which investors have access to financial information, including prices, market data, and financial reports. Transparency relating to information provided by companies is known as disclosure. Transparency is a prerequisite for free and efficient markets.

Trust. A situation where one party, known as the trustor, gives another party the right to hold assets for the benefit of a third party.

Unbanked. Slang terminology for people who do not use a bank or other financial institutions.

Welfare. A government program by which financial assistance is provided to individuals who cannot support themselves. Welfare programs are funded by taxpayers.

Will. A document specifying the distribution of a person's assets upon death.

Withholding. Part of an employee's wages that is not included in his or her paycheck because it is directly forwarded to federal, state, and local tax authorities.

Yield. The return on an investment, including interest or dividends received from a security. Usually expressed as an annual percentage calculated by dividing earnings by the initial investment.

SOURCES

Banks, Erik. *The Palgrave Macmillan Dictionary of Finance, Investment and Banking.* New York: Palgrave Macmillan, 2010.

Investopedia.com. "Dictionary." www.investopedia.com/dictionary/.

Jump$tart Coalition for Personal Financial Literacy. "National Standards in K-12 Personal Finance Education." 2007. http://jumpstart.org/assets/files/standard book-ALL.pdf.

Public Schools of North Carolina. "Personal Financial Literacy: Glossary of Commonly Used Terms." n.d. www.dpi.state.nc.us/pfl/students/glossary/.

RESOURCES

360 Degrees of Financial Literacy (American Institute of CPAs)

Website produced by American Institute of CPAs, this is a free program to help Americans understand their personal finances through various stages of life.

- https://www.360financialliteracy.org

BRASS Business Guides

BRASS (Business Reference and Services Section) of ALA's Reference and Services Association maintains LibGuides on a range of topics, including personal financial literacy.

- http://brass.libguides.com/financialliteracy

Consumer Financial Protection Bureau (CFPB)/Library Resources

Features programming ideas, graphics, and materials for download or to order in print, webinar archive for librarian training, and recommended websites. The broader website offers resources for consumers.

- https://www.consumerfinance.gov/practitioner-resources/library-resources/

Federal Deposit Insurance Corporation (FDIC) Money Smart, Financial Education Program

Launched in 2001 and regularly updated, Money Smart is a comprehensive financial education curriculum designed to help low- and moderate-income individuals outside the financial mainstream enhance their financial skills and create positive banking relationships.

- https://www.fdic.gov/consumers/consumer/moneysmart/

Federal Reserve Education

This site provides lesson plans, classroom activities, publications, and games as well as financial information for the general public, including credit, banking, personal finance, and consumer protection.

- www.federalreserveeducation.org

Institute for Financial Literacy

A nonprofit organization whose mission is to promote effective financial education and counseling. Founded in 2002, the institute accomplishes its mission by working with organizations to incorporate financial education into their existing services.

- https://financiallit.org

Investor.gov | Security and Exchange Commission (SEC)

From the SEC's Office of Investor Education and Advocacy, this site offers resources on investing wisely and avoiding fraud.

- https://www.investor.gov

Money Matters | New York Public Library

Money Matters is a series of workshops and e-learning modules created to help New York Public Library staff, other libraries, and not-for-profit organizations understand key personal finance concepts, subject-matter content, and available unbiased, research-based resources.

- https://sites.google.com/a/nypl.org/money-matters/

Money Smart Week

The website of the successful public awareness campaign well known to libraries and the many other organizations that participate.

- https://www.moneysmartweek.org

MyMoney.gov

US Treasury website with curriculum support and resources for teaching financial capability.

- https://www.mymoney.gov

National Endowment for Financial Education (NEFE)

NEFE, an independent, nonprofit foundation, offers a variety of self-help websites and resources that are noncommercial and frequently updated.

- https://www.nefe.org

Programming Librarian

A resource for programming ideas around a range of topics, from ALA's Public Programs Office.

- http://www.programminglibrarian.org

SaveAndInvest.org. FINRA Investor Education Foundation

Free, unbiased resource dedicated to helping people manage their finances safely and appropriately. The website has special sections with tools and information for helping military service members achieve their financial goals and for helping investors avoid investment fraud.

- https://www.saveandinvest.org

Smart investing@your library | ALA and FINRA Investor Education Foundation

Website to complement initiative to support library efforts to provide effective, unbiased financial education programs. Includes news on grant programs.

- https://smartinvesting.ala.org

INDEX